THE GOSPEL UNHINDERED

Modern Missions and the Book of Acts

Doug Priest Jr., editor

William Carey Library

PASADENA, CALIFORNIA

Published by
William Carey Library
P.O. Box 40129
Pasadena, CA 91114
(626)798-0819

ISBN 0-87808-256-5

Printed in the U.S.A.

Print-on-Demand Edition 2000

CONTENTS

CONTRIBUTORS

W. Michael Smith has worked as General Director of the Christian Missionary Fellowship since 1986. He served in Ethiopia and then Indonesia for a total of eleven years. His M.Div. is from Emmanuel School of Religion and he has completed classwork toward a D. Min. from Fuller Theological Seminary. "Mick" and Joyce have two children.

Jonathan Morse was raised in Burma as a third generation missionary. Now living in Thailand, Joni ministers through Bible translation, leadership development, village evangelism and materials production. A graduate of Pacific Christian College, Joni is currently enrolled in a Ph.D. program at Fuller Theological Seminary. Joni and Nangsar have three children.

Larry Griffin is a graduate of Mid-South Christian College and Fuller Theological Seminary. As a missionary with Team Expansion, he has been working in urban church planting in Montevideo, Uruguay since 1982. Larry and Ruth have one son.

Greg Johnson, son of missionary parents, was raised in Ethiopia. He has worked among the Maasai people in Kenya for sixteen years. Greg's M.Div. is from Emmanuel School of Religion and he has done further graduate studies in community development at the Univ. of Florida. Greg and Becky have two daughters.

David and Sheela Lall were born in India. David earned his Bachelor's degree from Jabalpur University, majoring in electronics and telecommunications. Sheela's Master's degree is in Psychology. Their primary work with the Mid India Christian Mission is in the area of evangelism and leadership training through the use of various media, including television, video, literature and radio. David and Sheela have three children.

Effie Giles served as a missionary in Ethiopia for eleven years. She then assisted her husband Ray as Field Director for Christian Missionary Fellowship for fifteen years, until their return to Ethiopia in 1992. She studied at Roanoke Bible College. She and Ray have four children.

Gail and Wayne Long began their ministry in Dallas, Texas. Later they served as missionaries for seven years in Brazil. They returned to the United States to found the Hisportic Christian Mission which has planted ten churches among Portuguese speaking people in the New England area. The Longs earned their M.Div's from Brite Divinity School and did further graduate studies at Fuller Theological Seminary. They have two sons.

Donald S. Tingle serves as Executive Director of CAS International, a ministry to the Muslim world, and as associate professor at Cincinnati Bible College and Seminary. His M.A. is from Hartford Seminary, and he is a Ph.D. candidate from Drew University. His most recent field research is among the Crimean Tatar. Don and Linda have four children.

Nangsar Sarip Morse is from the Rawang tribal group from Burma. Speaking seven different languages, she lives with her family in Thailand. Nangsar graduated from Pacific Christian College. Her ministry involves the training of Lisu and Lahu tribal leaders in Thailand in addition to producing leadership materials for the churches in Burma.

Frederick W. Norris, who earned his Ph.D. from Yale University, is Professor of Christian Doctrine at Emmanuel School of Religion. He served as Director of the Institute for Christian Origins in Tuebingen, Germany, and is currently editing 8 volumes entitled *Christianity in Its Religious Contexts*.

Doug Priest Jr. earned his Ph.D. from Fuller Theological Seminary following ten years as a missionary in Kenya and Tanzania. The son of missionary parents, Doug resides in Singapore where he serves as Asia Coordinator for Christian Missionary Fellowship. Doug and Robyn have two daughters.

Dennis Free graduated from Atlanta Christian College and Luther Rice Seminary. He has served as a missionary in Indonesia for nineteen years, where his work includes church planting and leadership development. Dennis and Lynn have two children.

Doug Lucas served as a missionary in Uruguay in 1982, and is now President of Team Expansion. Doug recently spent six months in the former Soviet Union to assist in opening new works among Ukrainians and Crimean Tatars. He graduated from Cincinnati Bible Seminary and is a Ph.D. candidate at California Coast University. Doug and Penny have two sons.

Carolyn Butler has been a missionary in Zaire since 1961 with African Christian Mission. Her work in benevolence, teaching, translation and writing has taken her across Zaire, where she has studied five different cultures. Carolyn and Ron have three children. She studied at Lincoln Christian College.

A. Wayne Meece served as a minister for many years before going to Liberia as a missionary. The Meece's were forced to evacuate Liberia due to the civil war after serving there for ten years. They are currently ministering in Ivory Coast. Wayne's M.Div. is from Lincoln Christian Seminary. Wayne and Greta have three children.

PREFACE

The final words of Jesus before His ascension into Heaven, usually termed the Great Commission, are related in different accounts in the Gospels. Their fruition begins to be chronicled in the book of Acts. The Acts of the Apostles is the primary missionary document of the New Testament. From its beginning in Jerusalem, the Gospel spreads through Judea, to Samaria and unto the uttermost parts of the world within the chapters of this book.

That the Gospel continues to spread throughout the world to this day is an historical fact. Christianity remains the world's most adhered to religion. Missionaries, evangelists and teachers continue to take inspiration from the mission themes found in the book of Acts. They are always taken aback by the relevance of the text, even after almost 2000 years.

Inspiration for *The Gospel Unhindered: Modern Missions and the Book of Acts* probably goes back twenty years to my mentor, Alan R. Tippett, who taught me a great many things about missions. He felt that the book of Acts often did not receive the recognition it deserves in the textbooks on Theology of Missions. Emphasis on the Son and on the Great Commission, while important of course, has tended too minimize the role of the Spirit and the Apostles.

Secondly, Tippett felt that many missionaries provide excellent comments on the text that might be missed by those who have never served in another cultural setting. They have to distill the Gospel to its essence and isolate it from its cultural expression in their home society when they present it in another. Their observations should be heard.

The chapters of this book each develop a different mission theme from the book of Acts. All are written by those who have spent years ministering in other cultures. Each author discusses how the theme is played out in today's world. The men and women who contributed to this book relate their mission experiences from five continents.

It is not possible to highlight every mission theme from the Acts of the Apostles. Space prohibits, for example, articles on the subjects of healing, missionary preparation or overcoming the tension in the early church between Jew and Gentile.

I wish to thank others who have assisted in the preparation of this book. The staff of William Carey Library has been most helpful, and special appreciation goes to Don Nickles, Robyn Priest, Marge Priest and Chuck Hammond.

The unhindered spread of the Gospel was Luke's passion in writing Acts. It is my passion in providing this book. May it be the passion of the Church facing the new millennium.

1

PEACE AND HOPE TO ALL

by W. Michael Smith

Although Acts is a wonderful resource for personal growth, it is not your average self-help book. It is about God's agenda, not the agenda of someone whose interests are limited to his or her own family, race, region or political persuasion. The chapters in this book will draw you further into God's eternal purpose to bring the healing, peace and hope to all the peoples of the world.

God intends, through the work of his people who are filled with the Spirit of Christ, to bring healing to broken bodies and spirits, hope to those who are ground down and discouraged, justice to those who have been trampled by the more powerful, peace to brothers and sisters who are destroying one another in selfishness and anger, as well as forgiveness and eternal life to all. Acts recounts the struggle of Christians in the first century to move beyond the walls of self-interest to be partners with God in his effort to heal and renew his creation.

Serving the mission of God does not seem to come easy for us. In fact, God finds in many of us an array of hindrances to doing his work, especially in modern individualistic oriented America. In his book, Wild Hope, Tom Sine warns that many of us conservative Christians are guilty of a serious distortion which places "the individual, rather than God, at the center of the gospel. From this viewpoint, instead of Christians being co-conspirators in God's agenda of redeeming the world, God becomes a co-conspirator in their agenda of getting what they want out of life. God is there to help them get ahead in their careers, acquire their house in the suburbs, improve their relationships and 'color them beautiful' " (Sine 1991:198).

If the idea of learning to be a co-laborer with God interests you, read on. But realize that you will be joining a long list of believers through the ages who have taken the arduous challenge to translate that general desire into specific action. You will find in the pages of Acts familiar sounding struggles as devout Jewish Christians, guided by the Holy Spirit, agonized when they found in themselves a deeply rooted resistance to reaching out with a family kind of love to people that their culture, and even their religion, had told them were unworthy.

Their struggles parallel many we face today. How can we, as the people of God, show and tell God's love to such a culturally diverse and rapidly changing world? While we acknowledge that, in theory, people who are different than us are acceptable to God, the fact is our congregations seldom reflect much ethnic and social diversity. It was simple enough as children to sing "Jesus loves the little children...red and yellow, black and white..." It is not so simple, though, as adults, to know how to demonstrate God's love to people so different. It is hard enough to minister to people of our own ethnic and socioeconomic background, let alone the people of the world's ethnic mosaic.

The Lord has given to us, his church, the task of heralding Good News to all people. If you are thinking that sounds like a missionary task, you are right. And if you are a Christian, you share responsibility for that task, even if you do not see yourself as the missionary type.

When the church needs help to cope with change and diversity, the book of Acts in a good place to turn. In Acts we often see the Lord as teacher. He is teaching his followers how to be both faithful and flexible in changing times.   We mistakenly tend to think that faithfulness means hanging on tenaciously to the status quo. In Acts, faithfulness required Jesus' disciples to turn loose rather than hang on. The Holy Spirit persistently guided them to release their misconceptions about who God can love and accept. It was wrenching for them to lay aside a life time of unquestioned beliefs about who could be considered clean, holy and chosen by God. Now this radical Messiah was trying to teach them that God accepts and loves all people without partiality--and they must, too.

The church was born into turmoil and spent its first 30 years in a struggle to both establish its identity and survive in an increasingly hostile climate. Its leaders were faced with the same task Christian leaders still have to address today--they had to make sure they understood what the heart of the Good News was, and how God wanted the church to live in a radically changing cultural context. They were finding that being devout believers in God did not look like it did when they were growing up. The church today must also be dynamic and flexible if it is to faithfully serve the mission of Christ.

Throughout Acts we see the risen Christ, through his Holy Spirit, persistently teaching his church how to connect with the hurting peoples of this world, especially those who were ethnically and religiously different than the original believers. It may well be that the most important on-going ministry of God's Holy Spirit today is to teach his church how to embody God's love for all people, especially those our culture and even our religion have labeled untouchable or unworthy.

Who Wrote Acts?

While a few scholars have speculated otherwise, the consensus of both tradition and contemporary scholarship is that the physician Luke, the traveling companion of the Apostle Paul, was the author of the two volume work we call Luke and Acts. He drew on the wealth of his own experience and that of eyewitnesses of Christ's ministry to produce this account of what the Lord "continued to do and teach" through his church. Acts is far more than a stenographer's spartan account of activities. It is a masterful literary, historical and theological work. A well educated and gifted Gentile writer--from Antioch in Syria, according to tradition--Luke possessed a mastery of the Greek language unparalleled among New Testament writers.

Through his travels with the Apostle Paul, Luke was himself an eyewitness of many of the events he reports, as evidenced by the "we" passages of the book (Acts 16:10-17; 20:5-21:18; 27:1-28:16). He certainly must have used those long journeys as opportunity to learn from Paul about many events which transpired before Luke joined his missionary band. Furthermore, Luke had the benefit of personal interviews with other apostles and disciples, perhaps even Mary the mother of Jesus, and James the half-brother of Jesus. Luke may have learned about many of the events he reports in the first seven chapters of Acts from Peter's first hand account. He likely had access to the written record we call Mark's Gospel and other written compilations of events and teachings surrounding the Lord's ministry, death, resurrection and the early years of the life of the Church.

Luke probably composed Acts over a period of time and concluded it between A.D. 63-70. By knowing that Festus, the Governor of Palestine under whom Paul was sent to Rome, succeeded Felix in the winter of A.D. 55-56, then adding two years that Paul was clearly in Rome before the end of Acts, we can see that Acts was not written before A.D. 59 or 60. The absence of any references to the fall of Jerusalem in A.D. 70 suggests that Luke concluded his writing of Acts prior to that time. Some believe Acts was even written a little before the persecution of Christians in Rome in A.D. 64.

The Missionary Purpose at the Heart of Acts

Scholars have given a lot of attention to identifying why Acts was written. The modern title 'Acts of the Apostles' is misleading. Luke did not use that title for it at all. In fact, he gave it no title. He simply noted that it was a sequel to his earlier account of the life and ministry of Jesus. It was not until the fourth century AD that this document began to be called Acts of the Apostles. In addition, this work does not really give much attention to any of the apostles except Peter and Paul. All of the apostles are listed in the first chapter, but notice that after that, James gets one sentence, John is mentioned briefly, and even Peter fades from prominence after chapter 12. It does not seem that Luke's purpose was to give a detailed account of the lives and work of the apostles.

Luke addresses this volume, as he did his gospel, to Theophilus. His use of the term "most excellent" (Lk 1:3) hints that Theophilus was of high social rank. He was probably a believer, for Luke explains that he is writing so that "...you may know the certainty of the things you have been taught" (Lk 1:4). That same basic reason for writing applies to Acts just as it did to the Gospel of Luke.

Since Luke authored both volumes, we have to ask what distinctive purposes he had in mind in adding the second. His literary style suggests that he had more in mind than a simple historical record of the beginnings of Christianity. In Acts, Luke addresses several important purposes which were of critical importance for the church in his day and remain so for our generation.

1. Acts, especially when combined with the Gospel of Luke, provides for the church its primary historical narrative. The story of the

life of Christ and the unfolding church continues the narrative, begun in the Old Testament, of God's calling and work with the Hebrew people. Luke's two volumes show that God's intention in calling the Hebrew people was, after all, to bless all the nations of the world. His use of a style of Greek similar to that of the Septuagint, the Greek translation of the Old Testament, hints that Luke regarded himself as writing sacred history.

From the vantage point of this narrative we are able to watch the fulfillment of the covenant God made with Abram (Gen 12:1-3) that through his family--the people Israel--God would bless all the peoples of the world. Acts gives us the background for understanding Paul's letters, all of which are missionary in nature, reaching beyond Israel in fulfillment of God's promise for all the world.

2. Luke shows us in Acts that the essential task of the church is mission. We find very little about the inner life and workings of the church in Acts. Luke's major point is that the church, born in Judaism, fulfills God's intention for Israel by taking the light of his salvation to the Gentiles--to all peoples of the world. God's love embraces Jews and Gentiles, *ta ethne*, all of the world's people. His salvation must not be hoarded for Israel alone. In the early life of the church we witness the Holy Spirit helping the apostles overcome the prejudices, beliefs and assumptions which would have kept this movement a sect of Judaism. Many of the same factors obstruct the missionary work of Christ's church today.

Acts makes sure we understand that the mission of the Church in the world is unfinished. The church exists by mission just as a fire exists by burning. Mission is the essential nature of the church.

3. Acts also traces the geographical spread of the gospel. The narrative opens with a group of confused Jewish disciples of Jesus who have been told to wait in Jerusalem. Nevertheless, from the parting words of Jesus in 1:8, we recognize a plan for the proclamation of the Good News from that hub of Jerusalem all the way to the ends of the earth. Still, the geographic expansion was probably not Luke's primary purpose even though there is an obvious progression from Jerusalem outward throughout Palestine, into Syria, Asia Minor and on to Rome. For example, the point of Luke's account of Paul's journey to and arrival in Rome was not likely just to show that the gospel reached Rome since the Gospel came to Rome twenty years before Paul did.

4. Acts helped believers of the late first century by verifying that Paul and the others were true Apostles of Jesus Christ. Some first century critics had suggested that they corrupted the message of Christ. But we learn in Acts that they are, in fact, obedient disciples of Jesus Christ. We can count on their teaching and can trust that their practice of including non-Jews in the church is consistent with the will and teaching of Jesus.

5. The role of the Holy Spirit in Acts is so prominent that some suggest that "The Acts of the Holy Spirit" would be a better title than "The Acts of the Apostles." The Holy Spirit guided and empowered the church for its mission. Without the Holy Spirit, that band of followers would have faded into powerless, purposeless insignificance. But in the power of the Spirit, they turned the world upside down.

But we must see the ministry of the Holy Spirit in its context in Acts. The Holy Spirit was not sent to become a power source for self-serving use by the followers of Christ, not merely to upgrade the spiritual maturity of individual believers. In Acts, the Holy Spirit's presence is always associated with the mission of Christ. The Holy Spirit fulfills the promise to be a counselor by persistently guiding and teaching the young church so that it can comprehend and cooperate with the universal scope of the mission of Christ. That requires vigilance on the part of the Holy Spirit. The early Jewish believers encountered in themselves biases, assumptions and convictions which threatened from the outset to derail their obedience to the mission of Christ that was becoming clearer to them. But the Holy Spirit was unrelenting in his efforts to open the eyes of the believers and guide them to continue the work of Christ. Every miracle served to encourage new steps of missionary enterprise. Every vision led to wider proclamation of the Gospel. Every occasion of the gift of tongues signaled a new ethnic or geographic horizon for the spread of the Word.

The Holy Spirit is, then, the Spirit of the risen Christ, working to teach and empower the church to continue the work of making disciples among all peoples. Henry Martyn, the early missionary to India, once said that the Spirit of Christ is the spirit of missions. The nearer we get to him, the more intensely missionary we will become.

6. While we have noted several significant contributions that Luke made by writing Acts, it seems that his primary purpose was to show how God fulfills his intention to bring salvation to all peoples of

the world in spite of the hindrances that would have blocked God's purposes.

In the grace and power of the risen Christ, the people of God are able to overcome racial, religious and national barriers to fulfill the purpose for which God called Israel and the church into being. Taught and empowered by the Spirit of Christ, God's church is able now to be the agent of healing, hope and salvation for all the peoples of the world. It is here that God begins to "unbabel" the nations. Remember that God's covenant with Abram (Gen 12) with its promises to bless all the nations, follows immediately after the Tower of Babel experience (Gen 11) where sin led to the scattering of the nations. God's plan of salvation is not limited to individual forgiveness and transformation. It is God's intention, through the church, to transform families, communities, nations and the world.

The church is to model for the world what some consider a sociological impossibility--a community of men and women of tremendous ethnic, national and socioeconomic diversity unified in a new humanity that transcends what long seemed natural and insurmountable barriers to community.

Several scholars see Luke's use of the word koluo, translated as "hinder" or "forbid," as epitomizing the key message Luke wanted to convey in Acts. In Jesus, the Christ, there is life for all--all hindrances are removed. When the eunuch had learned from Philip that Jesus is the Messiah of whom Isaiah spoke, he asked, "what hinders me from being baptized?" (Acts 8:36 RSV). His was a question of acceptability. He was an Ethiopian, a Gentile, who knew that his access to Judaism was restricted. When Peter saw the Holy Spirit fall upon Cornelius and his household, he was forced to ask, "Can anyone hinder these people from being baptized with water?" (10:47 RSV). He was asking about acceptability because Cornelius and family were Gentiles. Was it permissible for them to drink of the water of life without fully becoming Jews first? When Peter recounted this startling development to the Apostles and brothers in Jerusalem the question was, "...who was I to think that I could hinder (oppose) God?" (11:17). Obviously it was God who had taught Peter not to call unclean what God had made clean. It was God who sent messengers ahead of the Gentile Cornelius to warn Peter that they would be coming, and it was God who astonishingly poured out his Spirit on uncircumcised Gentile hearers (10:45). God unquestionably intended to embrace the Gentiles without their becoming Jews. On what ground then should Peter or any of God's people reject God's obvious leading?

Acts shows the agonizing struggle of Jewish followers of Christ to believe that God could accept the uncircumcised. These disciples still saw themselves as a part of Judaism. Their religious leaders were the ones who had insisted that only the circumcised were acceptable to God. Now it had begun to appear that God was setting aside those requirements which would hinder the peoples of the world from enjoying the full blessing of life through faith in God's Messiah. Summing it all up, Luke chooses to conclude Acts with an adverb which becomes the powerful final chord of his orchestral masterpiece: "Boldly and without hindrance he preached the kingdom of God and taught about the Lord Jesus Christ" (28:31).

On that word, literally, Luke's work is complete. The gospel of Jesus Christ is wonderful news to all the people of the world who finally may come to God, and to Life, without hindrance. It remains our task to so closely follow the Spirit of the Risen Christ that we do not hinder his work in our complex age.

Conclusion

The following liturgical reading clearly expresses the missionary purpose of the book of Acts. It is adapted from an article by James Reapsome (1993:28:24:8).

A Reading about How We See

Leader: Whites are better than blacks.
People: All humans are created in the image of God.

Leader: Men are better than women.
People: All humans are created in the image of God.

Leader: Jews are better than Palestinians.
People: God has no favorites.

Leader: The rich are better than the poor.
People: God does not show partiality.

Leader: Those never divorced are better than the divorced.
People: All are fully loved and accepted by God.

Leader: Straights are better than gays.
People: God's grace extends to all sinners.

Leader: God values the young more than the old.
People: Every human is fully loved by God.

Leader: Luciano Pavorotti is better than Michael Jackson.
People: Every voice is a gift from God.

Leader: Americans are better than Iraqis.
People: God's grace extends to the people of every nation.

Leader: Those who live in the suburbs are better than those in the ghettos.
People: Christ was sent to release the oppressed.

Leader: Anglo-Saxons are better than Africans and Asians.
People: All nations will see God's glory.

Leader: Christians are better than Muslims and Hindus.
People: When Christ is lifted up all people are drawn to him.

Leader: The well fed are obviously more blessed by God than the hungry.
People: The Kingdom belongs to those who hunger for justice.

Leader: I now see how true it is that God has no favorites.
People: Our Creator God loves and cares for all people. The wonder of Christ is that by his Spirit, we can experience the impartial love of others and show even to those most different from us, the kind of love and care fit for family.

An Outline of Acts

2

IN THEIR OWN LANGUAGE

by Jonathan Morse

> *When they heard this sound, a crowd came together in bewilderment, because each one heard them speaking in his own language. Utterly amazed, they asked: "Are not all these men who are speaking Galileans? Then how is it that each of us hears them in his own native language?" (Acts 2:6-8).*

The Pentecost incident, as recorded in the second chapter of the book of Acts, can be rightly regarded as the watershed event of the New Testament Church. It was on this occasion that the full significance of Christ's death, burial and resurrection became clear, not only to Jesus' disciples, but also to many of the multitudes gathered in Jerusalem for the annual celebration of the Feast of Weeks.

An Early Exercise in Mission Strategy

According to the account given to us by Luke, there were in Jerusalem during this time God-fearing Jews from "every nation under heaven" (Acts 2:5). The place names given for these visitors' points of origin virtually encompassed the entire known world of that day. It was in this context that one of the most astonishing events of the New Testament era occurred.

Prior to Christ's ascension, he had instructed his disciples not to leave Jerusalem. They were to wait for the gift which was promised to them by the Father. Jesus told them, "John baptized with water, but in a few days you will be baptized with the Holy Spirit" (Acts 1:5).

Following Christ's instructions, the disciples, along with some of the other believers remained in Jerusalem and regularly joined together for prayer. When the day of Pentecost arrived, they were all together in one place.

Suddenly, we are told, a sound like the blowing of a violent wind came from heaven and filled the whole house where they were sitting. They saw what seemed to be tongues of fire that separated and came to rest on each of them. In an instant, all of them were filled with the Holy Spirit and began to speak in other tongues as the Spirit enabled them (Acts 2:2-4).

The unusual sound attracted a large crowd. Those who rushed to the scene to investigate the mid-morning commotion encountered something that would have a profound impact on their lives. The curious spectators stumbled upon what seemed to be a group of religious devotees boisterously declaring the wonders of God in a cacophony of regional tongues. Astonishingly, each person heard them speaking in his own native language!

What Does This Mean?

Naturally, all those who had witnessed this unusual event wanted to know what it was all about. Peter's explanation sheds much needed light on the significance of what happened on that day. In a very real sense, Pentecost can be correctly seen as marking the birthday of the early Church. And yet, Pentecost is so much more than a historical reference point. At Pentecost, God broke through our human language barriers and showed the world how to truly communicate.

Some commentators see an interesting link between Pentecost and Babel. The people whom God caused to be scattered over the face of the earth by confounding their language, were now being gathered to Himself through the instrumentality of the gift of languages given to the apostles.

The miracle of Pentecost shows us how important language is for the successful communication of the gospel. For every person present at that historic gathering in Jerusalem, God suddenly became very near and very real. The people were touched to the core of their being.

What was it that moved the audience with such conviction that day? There can be no doubt that it was through the appropriate use of language, accompanied by the confirming work of the Spirit that the apostles were able to penetrate the hearts of the people. It was through the facility of language that the early Christians were able to proclaim the message of Christ to the very ends of their known world.

The implication of this for us is enormous. If the modern Church has any desire to try to approximate the success of the first century Church, it will have to learn to appreciate the important role that language plays in the dissemination of the Christian faith.

Hearing the Gospel in One's Heart Language

The people who were gathered in Jerusalem on the day of Pentecost each heard the apostles declaring the wonders of God in their own "native language" (Acts 2:8). Most commentators agree that the word used here would also take into account the varieties of regional dialects that were spoken throughout the first century world.

If we accept Luke's account of what happened at Pentecost, we may safely assume that every person heard the apostles speaking in his or her own language. For the audience that day, it was clearly a miracle of supernatural proportions. For those of us removed from that experience by the elapsed centuries however, we must understand the phenomenon of Pentecost as our first lesson in effective Christian communication.

Cameron Townsend, the founder for Wycliffe Bible Translators, is said to have once been challenged by a person who asked him, "If God is so smart, why doesn't He speak my language?" This, of course, was precisely what God was doing at Pentecost. And this is what God still does wherever He has people who have seen the efforts to which God will go in order to make Himself understood.

A *heart language* is the language which people grow up speaking from childhood. It is the language of preference when family members speak to each other in their own homes. It is also the preferred language for anybody wanting to effectively communicate with others about spiritual matters.

If God is going to speak to people in their heart language today, it will have to be done through the mouths of Christian witnesses. That every person has a right to personally hear the Word of God in order to make an intelligent decision about Christ can hardly be disputed. Missionaries and Bible translators from the earliest times on down to the present have given their lives to make the scriptures available in the major languages of the world.

In spite of this tremendous effort, there still remain countless groups of people who have yet to hear about the good news of Jesus Christ, and of God's deep love for them. The emphasis on *Unreached Peoples* has come into existence around this one great need to proclaim Christ to those living beyond the immediate influence of the Church.

If the majority of these unreached people groups are to learn about the love of God now being expressed through His Son Jesus Christ, they will have to hear it presented to them in their own mother tongue. Seen in this light, the remaining task of proclaiming the gospel to the uttermost parts of the earth takes on a whole new perspective.

How then is this communication task to be undertaken? To be sure, God's people are going to have to double their efforts to bridge the enormous information gap that exists in this area. For starters, it will require Christians to pay increased attention to familiarizing themselves with the family trees of the world's major language groups.

Interest in unreached people groups will also have to become more than a passing fad, or the latest bandwagon for churches to climb aboard on. Realistically, the many well intended terms that are currently circulating among Christians, such as "Adopt a People," or "Adopt a City," will need to very soon become "Engage a People" and "Enter a City," if we are going to make a significant dent on this world. Great sounding slogans, though effective, can just as easily lull people to sleep if not acted upon.

The Messenger Becomes the Message

Communication theory has helped us to see that there is much that happens to a message from the time it leaves the sender to the time it reaches the receiver. A typical piece of information undergoes numerous transformations as it travels from person to person.

Perhaps each of us can remember the childhood game which involved a message to be whispered to a partner and then sent around the room from ear to ear. Almost without fail, the original message would get twisted beyond recognition. Something as simple as "Mary loves Peter," could easily become "Lucy is going to have a baby!" And this occurred when the same language is used--just imagine two or more languages in the process.

The message of Christ is no less vulnerable to this kind of distortion. This is one reason at least why so many bizarre beliefs and practices have sprouted up within supposedly Christian circles. It is downright frightening to realize how capable we are of churning out so much hogwash.

Yet, we also know that there is a sinister hand involved which is at work to complicate matters beyond our limited understanding. As so often seems to be the case, God breathes life, and we inhale death. He sends rain, and we receive fire. How are we to safeguard the message?

Fortunately, God has given us the Holy Spirit to help us process His Word. The Holy Spirit helps us with both the filtering as well as the transmitting tasks. He does this by actually residing within us in order to provide a distortion free message. As the apostle Paul has put it, "We have this treasure in jars of clay to show that this all-surpassing power is from God and not from us" (2 Co 4:7).

Mission in the Mind of God

It was God's intention from the very beginning to bless all the peoples of the world through the mission He assigned Abraham (Gen 12:1-3). This *peoples of the world* idea is a recurrent theme that runs throughout the Bible. God's love for the human family has always embraced the entire world. Even a cursory review of the Old Testament reveals ample evidence of God repeatedly calling Israel back to this plan of His--to bless all peoples on earth.

Yet the history of Israel shows how God's people continually turned inward, focusing on their own perceived needs. God wanted to live among His people in a tent, in order to travel with them, but the Israelites wanted God in a temple, so that He would stay put. God wanted to be their divine ruler, but they wanted their own earthly king. Many of the prophets of old talked themselves hoarse, only to be silenced with the sword by a people who no longer wanted to follow an agenda not of their own making.

Even with the coming of Jesus and His clear instructions about going into all the world, the early disciples of Christ had to literally be dislodged from Jerusalem by a great persecution n order to break up the church and scatter it among the nations.

This tendency to settle down and to send out roots is still very much with us. We would all rather stay put and tend to our own concerns, than to venture out into the unknown in pursuit of God's purposes.

The issue here is not so much about a surface response, but about a matter of the heart. God really is not all that interested in our going or not going somewhere for Him. He is much more eager to find out how willing we are to forsake all in order to follow after Him. God's deepest desire is for us to get on board. But He wants us to join him on the deck. To His way of thinking, if we want to remain below deck, then we might as well be asleep in the belly of a fish.

Roadside Encounters With God

The pattern of outreach which emerged in the early church is beautifully portrayed for us in the person of Philip the evangelist. We see in Philip a model communicator. Philip was one of the seven deacons chosen to serve the church in Jerusalem soon after its formation.

Philip is attested to have been a man "full of faith and of the Holy Spirit" (Acts 6:5). These qualifications, it seems, were quite sufficient to ignite the hidden power of the early church, thereby launching it on its divine mission to the world.

The account of Philip's encounter with the Ethiopian official illustrates perfectly what Christianity is all about-- one person introducing another to Christ the Savior (Acts 8:26-40). It is this simple *sharing* of the good news about Jesus and His love that has resulted in changed lives the world over. Dramatic changes can always be expected to occur whenever Jesus and His claims are brought to bear on life's issues.

The roadside teaching session demonstrates for us two very important approaches in sharing the gospel. Philip employed both personal testimony as well as the written scriptures in his interaction with the Ethiopian. Both the spoken word as well as the written word were used to great effect.

This first century example of effective Christian communication can serve as an important illustration for us as we too go about preaching Christ in our world today. Every serious attempt to evangelize a people group will have to make provision for these two components. The spoken word will need to be followed by the written word.

In a cross-cultural context, the communication process can be further complicated initially by the need to rely on local trade languages. Nevertheless, taking our cue from Pentecost, we should make every effort to move beyond the limitations of a trade language, in order to gain the kind of access to people available only through a heart language.

The Conversion of the Naga

The Naga people of Burma are located in the northwest corner of the country which borders with India. The famous Ledo Road, which was constructed during World War II, runs across the northern portion of Naga country connecting India with China. Following the British withdrawal from Burma in 1948, the Naga territory has remained largely unadministered. To this day, the area is practically inaccessible to outsiders.

The most recent information indicates that there are over eighty-five different Naga dialect groups packed into this area. The Burma side Naga population can be further differentiated into groups such as the Haimi Naga, the Lai Nawng Naga, the Tanghkul Naga, and the Makuri Naga, etc. Collectively, these various Naga sub-groups refer to themselves as Hawa Naga.

The Naga people being spotlighted here came into contact with the gospel in the early 1960s. Prior to that time, they were certified headhunters, feared throughout the region for their practice of human sacrifice. Nobody dared to travel throughout Naga territory without taking extreme precaution.

One winter afternoon in the early months of 1960, a small hunting party of Lisu Christians found themselves camped near the head waters of the Tarung River in northern Burma. Unwittingly, the band had wandered about two days journey into Naga country.

That evening, as was their customary practice before retiring for the night, the hunters brought out their hymnals which every Christian carried, and proceeded to have a prayer service on the banks of the picturesque river. Unknown to the Lisu Christians, a Naga war party had spotted them since early morning. After stalking them throughout the day, they finally had the hapless intruders completely surrounded.

The Naga warriors had noted many peculiarities about these particular strangers. They seemed to travel through the jungle with complete abandon. They exhibited no fear, and they took no precautions against possible attack. They posted no guard. The most astonishing thing, however, was their total disregard of the spirit world. None of the required rituals for warding off the evil spirits had been performed by the trespassers while setting up camp. They seemed oblivious to the many dangers that could be lurking in the dark.

Then, as the Naga headhunters were about to close in, the naive band of defenseless campers suddenly burst forth with clamorous singing. To the startled Naga, something had gone terribly wrong. This was absolutely unheard of. It was enough to make anyone's blood run cold.

The sounds which emanated out of that jungle prayer meeting echoed and reverberated up and down the narrow valley, completely ruining the Naga warrior's chances of a surprise attack. As far as the spirit world was concerned, this was definitely an inauspicious night for headhunting! They could not risk offending the spirits by adding commotion to this rude disturbance that awakened the whole night air.

As the Naga men crouched in the cover, a strange peace seemed to radiate out of the campsite. They could not help but notice the smiles on each camper's face, while terror gripped their own hearts. They were dumbfounded by the sheer joy and laughter being displayed by the singers. The Naga slowly retreated in order to regroup. They decided that they had to further investigate these strange people before they did anything else.

The next morning, the Lisu experienced the fright of their lives. Their bleary eyes were greeted by the sight of two dozen menacing warriors all poised with spears in hand. Each Lisu froze where he had bolted upright. The lead Naga tore into the camp shouting in Jinghpaw, the trade language of the area. One of the Lisu Christians who had gone through the mission school quickly responded in Jinghpaw, and God saved the day.

The Naga were full of questions. They wanted to know who the strangers were. Why were they not afraid of the spirits? How could they travel through the jungle with such ease and set up camp so casually? What were they so happy about? Did they know whose territory they were in? What was last night's singing all about?

By midmorning, the Naga warriors were sitting by the water's edge, and a providential evangelistic meeting was in full session. The Naga headhunters were converted on the spot. When the extended exchange ended, they demanded that this good news be presented to their people as well. Glancing around, the Lisu Christians realized that they were in no position to refuse. They told the Naga men that most of them had families that they needed to get back to. They could not just disappear like this. If they did not return to their own villages, a search party would most likely come looking for them.

The Naga were not to be dissuaded. They insisted that the Lisu group follow them to their villages which were located three days' journey further downstream. The Lisu felt their stomachs knot up as a sinking sensation washed over them. Were they being lured into a treacherous trap?

As the Naga were not budging from their demand, the Lisu finally agreed to let two of their party go with the Naga if in exchange, the Christians could take back with them two of the Naga men as well. This was the only way of showing good faith to each other. At last, the Naga agreed to the proposal.

Both of the Lisu men who were taken by the Naga hunting party went on to become full time missionaries among the Naga. The two young Naga men who accompanied the Lisu Christians back to their homes in the Putao Valley were put through an intensive program of training.

Gertrude Morse, my grandmother, provided the two with a solid grounding in the Scriptures. Her son and my father, Robert Morse, worked on an orthography for their language and produced a simple primer and song book in Naga.

After receiving several months of practical training in various areas, the two young men returned to their own people in the company of four Lisu and Rawang missionary families. Today, one of those first two Naga men heads up the Naga Bible translation team, which has recently completed work on the New Testament. The missionary outreach to the Naga has resulted in over 10,000 Christians being added to the church in some sixty villages.

The Frustrations of Literature Production

In 1960 Robert Morse produced the first written script for the Moshang-Lunghi dialect speakers of the Naga language. With the help of the two Naga language informants who had themselves just recently turned to Christ, he put together a simple Christian primer consisting of some basic Christian teaching materials along with some songs for the new Christians to learn. Armed with this teaching aid, the Rawang and Lisu Christian churches of the Putao plains in North Burma sent out four missionary families to evangelize the Naga of the upper Tarung valley.

Fifteen Naga villages turned to the Lord as a result of that early work. A few years later, the newly established Naga churches sent some of their young men to Putao to study the scriptures and to receive training for Christian ministry. Many of these young Timothys went on to become qualified preachers among their own people, and continue to serve their churches faithfully.

However, while the churches managed to experience some significant gains, a number of circumstances brought all work on Naga literature production to a virtual standstill. Chief among these circumstances was the political unrest that engulfed North Burma starting in the mid 1960s. Although a Naga literature committee was formed in 1970, they were unable to produce anything until 1977, when 270 copies of an updated version of the original primer was printed.

In 1983, the churches in Putao helped print 300 copes of an expanded second edition of the primer. This was the extent of the literature being produced for the Naga churches. For a growing church, which at the time numbered between four to five thousand Christians, this was clearly inadequate. Yet the churches themselves felt that they were not capable of producing the kind of quality materials needed for church-wide use among the many Naga sub-groups.

Realizing this, the Naga churches decided to send out representatives to make contact with their former missionaries in order to inform them of the various needs faced by the Naga churches. One of the men, elder Lawnhkan, was one of the two original language informants who assisted Robert Morse back in 1960.

In May 1984 church elder Lawnhkan and his companion Win Lum arrived in Thailand to establish contact with members of the North Burma Christian Mission which was now serving in Thailand. The two men brought with them a letter from the Naga churches requesting assistance in meeting their pressing literature needs. Accordingly, work on the Naga New Testament project was begun in June 1984 under my supervision.

The project began with an analysis of the Naga language and the introduction of a new orthography. A translation team was then formed with personnel who were handpicked by the Naga church leaders themselves. In order to better facilitate communication, it was decided that the team be based on the Thai-Burma border. The translation team has stayed in touch with the Naga churches through frequent return trips. These visits helped to establish a language committee to oversee the progress of the work.

The Naga Bible translation project proceeded to advance with record speed. After the translation team was exposed to some of the problems and principles of Biblical exegesis and translation concerns, the work took off with almost a life of its own. To assist them in the work, the team has relied primarily on other Bible translations already available in a number of regional languages.

Although the translation of the Naga New Testament was completed *within a period of only five years*, the work again became sidelined for lack of sufficient printing funds. This has practically canceled out any gains that have been made by the effort to find a more satisfactory approach to Bible translation work. One of the Naga team has asked, "If it is really this difficult, then what is the point of trying?"

Rethinking Bible Translation Work

Thirty-four years is a long time for a people to have to wait. This is how long the Naga of northern Burma have waited for the scriptures to be translated into their language. Although in their case, much of the down time can be blamed on the political turmoil and civil unrest which went on within the country, this is not an untypical delay in the world of Bible translation. In fact, the experience of the Naga people is more likely to be the norm rather than the exception in this line of work.

In actuality, a period of three to four decades is not an uncommon time-frame for most Bible translation projects. Sadly, this has become an acceptable benchmark for measuring progress in the Bible translation field. An examination of this problem however, reveals a number of factors that have contributed to this very unsatisfactory situation.

One of the existing roadblocks in the field of Bible translation has been the traditional perception that has viewed Bible translation work as a career occupation reserved only for the specially trained missionary. Of necessity, Bible translation work does indeed require the skills of highly qualified and dedicated individuals. At minimum, this has usually meant that a candidate acquired training in biblical studies and linguistics. Beyond that, the sky was the limit as to what a would-be translator wanted to arm him or herself with.

Of course, such a perspective immediately eliminates a large slice of the potential Bible translation population. To begin with, most people find that their nerve endings start going numb at the mere mention of grammatical classifications such as phonemes and morphemes. Start discussing categories such as syntax or transactional analysis and you've put your listener into deep freeze! Compound this with descriptions of a few other tongue twisters, pharyngeal stops, lateral clicks, and you have completely lost your dear friend.

Such a specialized approach to missionary preparation has inevitably caused many to look at the Bible translation profession with reverent awe. This sense of mystery attached to translation work has been further reinforced by the personal testimonies of Bible translators themselves. Many have been rumored to be able to rattle off at least a dozen foreign languages without the slightest effort.

As a result, many have come to assume that Bible translation work can only be done by a select group of highly trained people. Nothing could be further from the truth. Such an erroneous view can only serve to discourage Christians from considering what their own contribution could be in furthering this extremely important task.

Another factor that has seriously hindered the progress of Bible translation work is the funding bottleneck that has been created by the Church itself. By funneling most, if not all of its donations earmarked for Bible printing through the few existing Bible Society conglomerates, the Church has inadvertently put the brakes on the spread of grassroots Bible translation projects around the world.

The lack of funding has deterred many a capable group from undertaking a well organized translation project. In most cases, the need for an adequate translation project has been long overdue. Many people groups who are in the midst of turning to the Lord en masse, are in desperate need of the scriptures in their own languages.

Unfortunately, this is where some major shortcomings show up in the present Bible distribution system.

For all the good that they have done for the advancement of Christianity, Bible Societies today may be in danger of becoming unwieldy monopolies by default. In their zeal to become custodians of the scriptures, Bible Societies have been increasingly unwilling to touch any translation effort that has not received their particular stamp of approval. Some of the reasons given for this reluctance have to do with concerns for the accuracy of the overall translation, and its faithfulness to the original languages.

Yet, in spite of these reasonable precautions, the Bible Societies have not been able to demonstrate their ability to cover all the bases adequately. While concern for accuracy and faithfulness to the original languages of transmission are laudable guidelines, failure to devise more effective means for delivering the scriptures to the many people groups still waiting in the winds is clearly unacceptable.

Because of their far reaching influence, these powerful instruments of the Church can no longer remain inflexible with the financial resources which God has placed at their disposal. Bible Societies must more actively seek to enlist the participation of both existing missionaries as well as national churches in the effort to provide the scriptures to the unreached people groups of the world. Only a collaboration of this scale can hope to undergird global evangelism.

Summary

The gift of language can be viewed either as a blessing or as a curse, depending on which side of the great divide one happens to be standing. The ability for two people to enter into meaningful conversation is an enriching experience. Drawing a complete blank from the other person while trying to seriously communicate, on the other hand, can be extremely discouraging. Learning to negotiate the rocky ground between comprehension and ignorance has always been the challenge in the human equation.

The unveiling of Christ's master plan at Pentecost paved the way for the Church to take the gospel to the uttermost parts of the world. The Jerusalem miracle, which enabled people to hear the good news about Jesus *in their own language*, turned the hearts of those first

Christians inside out. "What shall we do?" was the unanimous response of the multitudes as they came under the conviction of the Holy Spirit (Acts 2:37).

The entire history of the Church has been an attempt to repeat that first breakthrough made in Jerusalem. Since Pentecost, Christians the world over have been taking upon themselves the task of making known to others the story of Jesus and His love. Those who have been most successful in getting God's message across have learned to use the heart language of a people.

The Pentecost experience powerfully spotlights the central role that language plays in the cross-cultural communication of the gospel. Language has the unique ability to cut right through superficialities in order to get to the heart of matters. It has the capacity to sum up and give expression to life's pressing issues and concerns.

One crucial feature of language is that it requires a reliable vehicle for conveying it's message. Ironically, the meaning of every message is unavoidably influenced by the instrument used in the transmission process. For all intents and purposes, the messenger becomes the message. Thus, in any critique of the message, the messenger also receives an automatic evaluation.

Measuring missionary effectiveness is very important because *mission*, as understood in its widest application, is the primary instrument with which the Church goes about communicating the message of the cross. At the same time, what one chooses to measure is also important, as there are numerous areas in both life and ministry that seem to be of equal significance.

Because language plays such a vital role in facilitating the spread of Christianity, it is imperative that the Christian message be made available to people in both its spoken, as well as its written form. If this is to be realized, many of the methods, approaches and time-frames that have come to be widely accepted in Bible translation circles will need to be seriously reexamined. Roadblocks that currently exist in the literature production field will also need to be identified and removed.

It has been sufficiently demonstrated that nationals as well as expatriates with little or no background in biblical studies or linguistics are capable of initiating Bible translation projects with only a minimum of training and supervision. Empowering local people who have an interest in contributing to Bible translation work could potentially unleash a previously untapped resource within the Church.

Entrusting ownership of translation projects to a broader segment of the Church would allow Bible translation consultants to give more of their time to furthering their own knowledge of the key trade languages spoken within their areas of responsibility.   Such a reformulation of priorities would enable translation consultants to accomplish more as they coordinate regional grassroots translation teams.

If we are to learn anything from the parable of the sower, we will need to understand that the story is meant to provide the leading criteria for measuring success within the Kingdom of God (Mt 13). If this is so, then it behooves us to evaluate all our work in terms of what Christ Himself considers to be an acceptable return.

It has become increasingly apparent that far greater resources will need to be mobilized and committed to the twin tasks of Bible translation and Bible publication work, if people who have yet to be adequately evangelized are to receive God's Word. This will require Christians around the world to become more astute stewards of God's many gifts. As daunting a challenge as this may be, it is a path that must be taken if the remaining unreached people groups of the world are to hear the Word of the God in their own language.

3

SPIRITUAL FORMATION AS A MISSIONARY IMPERATIVE

by Larry Griffin

All the believers were one in heart and mind. No one claimed that any of his possessions was his own, but they shared everything they had. With great power the apostles continued to testify to the resurrection of the Lord Jesus, and much grace was upon them all. There were no needy persons among them. For from time to time those who owned lands or houses sold them, brought the money from the sales and put it at the apostle's feet, and it was distributed to anyone as he had need (Acts 4:32-35).

Have you ever been to a church where on the surface everything appeared to be going well, yet with further observation something seemed to be missing? People are being brought to the Lord, prayers are being offered, the Lord's supper is observed faithfully, Bible studies are being taught for every age level, and a full program of Christian activities is taking place. Yet, for some reason, there seems to be a void. Something is lacking, something that seems to elude our consciousness, yet it is very noticeable. More than likely the church is going through all of the motions, yet spiritual formation is not taking place.

Relating Church Planting and Spiritual Formation

How does spiritual formation fit into the tasks of a modern church planting missionary? Maybe we should first ask, "What does it

mean to be a 'church planting' missionary?" With the expansion of the
"Church Growth" school of thought in missionary circles, there has been
a renewed emphasis on the need to send out missionaries who are
"church planters" above all else. But what does that mean, exactly? If
a missionary desires to be a church planter, does it mean that all social
outreach programs and educational activities must be renounced in order
to concentrate all efforts on purely evangelistic enterprises? And, what
does evangelism mean? Is it simply bringing people to conversion, or
does it include discipleship? Is a church planted by bringing together
a group of people who have been converted, and then organizing that
group into an efficiently managed church organization?

If we do not recognize the significant role of spiritual formation
in the missionary process, we run the risk of establishing a multitude of
church groups, while finding that these groups lack the dynamic,
spiritual power of the church found in the book of Acts. Acts is an
historical record where everything takes place in the extreme. When
church growth occurs, it occurs in astounding numbers. When the Spirit
begins to work powerfully, He does so with incomprehensible force.
When the enemy attacks, it is with such cruelty that one staggers at the
thought of such persecution. When Luke describes the community
nature of the church, and expresses the love that they displayed, he does
with examples so extreme that scholars for centuries have wondered just
how practical this life really is. Yet, this dynamic spiritual formation
of the church in the book of Acts is a divinely inspired example of the
nature of a true community of believers.

Brought into the Kingdom of God

Christ's church was never intended to be just another group of
people with a different set of beliefs. Likewise, it is not the task of the
missionary to simply transfer a basic knowledge of religious facts or
doctrines to people who previously believed other sets of religious facts
or doctrines. The task of a true church planter must be to bring people
into a vibrant, powerful, radical way of life in the kingdom of God.
The parables of Jesus, the miracles he performed, and the lifestyle of his
followers in the gospels all point to the fact that Jesus' message was a
call to a radical, difficult, and totally different way of life. When he
called someone to follow him, it was a call to take up a cross, crucify
all that one once held dear, renounce life as it had been known up to

that time, and with a leap of faith follow the King of Kings into a new lifestyle.

The church we read about in the book of Acts knew this, and their experience stands today as a testimony that true spiritual formation in the kingdom of God is a radically transforming experience.

The Early Church in Jerusalem

The early church in Jerusalem is certainly not simply a group of people who have come together to hear sermons and lessons on a new doctrinal reality, rather it is a community in the fullest sense of the word. Before the Pentecost experience, these persons were a varied multitude of peoples from different parts of the world, with different occupations, different languages, and different family relations. Now, however, they have been molded into a solid, unified community of believers which is striving to live out on a practical level the principles of kingdom living learned from their Lord, Jesus Christ.

Many things strike us from this passage: the amazing display of unselfish love on the part of those who held possessions, the powerful testimony of the apostles about the resurrection of the Lord Jesus Christ, the grace that was upon the community of believers, and the tremendous sense of unity found among such a diverse group of people. We might ask, "Was it the powerful testimony of the resurrection of Jesus that brought about such unity, or was it the tremendous sense of community that made it possible to testify powerfully of the resurrection? Was it the marvelous display of love that brought down God's grace upon the believers, or was it this grace that made possible the unselfish displays of love?

In a certain sense these questions could be seen as the perennial question of which came first, the chicken or the egg? However, as we reflect upon the missionary task of taking the gospel to the whole world, these questions become not merely academic, but rather real, vitally important questions of priorities. Do we concentrate on preaching the resurrection of Jesus Christ, with the hope that a vital community life will result, or do we concentrate on developing a sense of community, love and justice in order to create an environment receptive to the message of salvation?

Most commentators on this passage underline the fact that the practice of sharing possessions and contributing to a communal style of life was not the norm, and was probably limited to the unique circumstances of the early Jerusalem church. The believers who came to form part of this community were Jews from different parts of the world, many of whom probably left everything to become a part of this movement. The need for economic aid and a more communal lifestyle would be obvious in this unique situation, but would not necessarily be repeatable under other circumstances.

It is also important to note that this was an utterly spontaneous response of love that was in no way dictated by the community, but rather manifested itself in voluntary contributions. Peter's response to Ananias and Sapphira when they wished to participate in the contribution of money makes it clear that it was not obligatory (Acts 5:3-4).

In a strongly capitalistic society like the United States, and in a culture that so fervently promotes the freedom of individual choice in economic matters, this contextualized interpretation of the text is probably important, but unfortunately it tends to obscure the more fundamental realities of this early Christian experience. The central theme of this passage, is not so much the economic reality as it is the unbelievable sense of unity that arose.

The passage says that "all the believers were one in heart and mind" (Acts 4:32). The word here used for "heart" is the common Greek term kardia, and the word used for "mind" is the term psuche, which is also often translated "soul". The use of these two words is probably not so much to distinguish two different aspects of the unity of the believers as it is to underline that in the very center of their being, these believers were one. The words heart, kardia, and mind psuche, are used throughout the New Testament as being the seat of both one's emotions and reason. This seat is the center of one's thoughts, desires, purposes and decisions. This is most clearly seen in the well known pronouncement of Jesus, "Love the Lord your God with all your heart and with all your soul and with all your mind" (Mt 22:37). The important point here is that the multitude of believers was one in its very center, or its very essence.

Principles of Unity in the Jerusalem Church

Something had happened to change these people. Their entrance into the church was not seen as an appendage to their everyday activities, but rather became a totally new reality for them. Their world was turned upside down. They left one kingdom and entered another. They were now literally brothers and sisters in a new family, and each one placed his or her loyalty in a common authority, the King of Kings, Jesus Christ. What was it that united them so intimately?

They Believed

First of all, we find that they believed. They were one, because a common faith united them. The text says, "all the believers were one..." This is not a simple, intellectual assent to a certain set of beliefs, but rather a heartfelt confidence or trust. This trust was placed in Jesus Christ, and was directed to Him as Lord. The text states that the apostles proclaimed powerfully "the resurrection of the Lord Jesus." The concept of "lord" was not lost on the early Christians. When Peter first proclaimed the gospel message, it was not an emphasis on Jesus as a Savior, nor on the necessity of receiving His forgiveness for sins, but rather that the resurrection of Jesus Christ proved that he was both Lord and Christ. The term "lord" might better be understood in contemporary times with words like "boss," "owner," or even "king." It is a concept of authority. The one who is "lord" has total and unquestioned authority, and can direct the behavior of his "subject" in every area of life.

The popular saying goes, "Too many cooks spoil the broth." If too many people are in positions of authority there will not be a coherence of action and the unity of an organization will be lost. This did not take place in the early church because they were all believers in Jesus Christ as the one and only Lord of their lives. He was not only their savior, saving them from a life of sin and leaving them to continue on, but rather was their king, giving them direction, and controlling their behavior. They lived out this new life with one heart and with one mind because they had one Lord.

They Experienced Much Grace

Secondly, their unity was possible because they experienced "much grace." Parker says, "The essence of the doctrine of grace is that God is for us" (1960:257). God looked favorably upon his church, and he felt joy. His people knew that God was happy, and they experienced his love, which in turn produced joy in their own lives. They did not sell their possessions and give to the poor because the law demanded it or because they were afraid of God's wrath if they did not give generously, but rather they acted out of the security that comes from knowing that God is pleased. God was happy, they were happy and the people around them were happy. The Christians enjoyed "the favor of all the people," leading us to believe that the early Christian community was one loved and respected by those who were not members of it. This does not mean that persecution and difficulty was foreign to their experience. However, the persecution was of the type that comes to a group precisely because it is experiencing success and popularity among the people.

Unity is practically impossible without this insulating sense of grace. When a group feels that no one, not even God, is on their side, they begin to bicker and fight among themselves and destroy any sense of unity other than that which is strictly imposed by an authoritarian leader. However, when a group lives in an environment of grace, feeling and knowing that God is with them, loves them, and is pleased with their life, they are able to withstand any persecution or problem because united they feel secure.

They Had Strong Leaders

Thirdly, the believers were one in heart and mind because they had strong, dependable and spiritual leaders. The text says that the apostles preached the word powerfully, and these same leaders distributed the material wealth that had been donated to those who had need. Although each believer was equipped to minister in powerful ways, there was a clearly respected leadership among the apostles. The church looked to them for direction.

Strong spiritual leadership is necessary for any congregation that desires the unity present in the early church. Luke's historical record of the growth of the church underlines that importance, and shows us the leadership of the apostles in the preaching of the word, the organization of the local assemblies, the resolution of doctrinal questions and the expansion of the church into regions previously unreached.

Faith Translated into Action

Finally, we must say that the early church had a tremendous sense of unity because their faith was translated into practical action.

Naturally the early church's message was strong in doctrinal content and was firmly based upon the truth of the scriptures. The apostles powerfully preached the resurrection of Jesus, which was the foundation of the gospel message. However, that message was more easily accepted by many simply because they could look at the lives of the early believers and see with their own eyes that Jesus truly had become their Lord and Christ. The generosity and love of the early Christian community gave testimony to the validity of their message. This was no mere indoctrination of philosophical arguments, but rather a radical transformation of life and a full acceptance of the principles of life in the kingdom of God. An emphasis on theological and doctrinal discussion produces division as differences of opinion arise and become important. But a life of unselfish love produces peace, harmony and unity.

So the early Christian church was not just a group of people who went through the motions of singing hymns, saying prayers, taking the Lord's Supper and preaching doctrines, but rather was a vital, living community full of Spiritual life that manifested itself in unity and love.

Quantity or Quality?

That brings us once again, however, to the question with which we began, "Which comes first, the sense of community and love or the acceptance of doctrinal truths?" As we have already pointed out this question becomes even more vital with the emphasis of the church growth movement on the sending of missionaries who specialize in evangelism and conversion, over and above formation of the spiritual life of the church once established. Many missionaries today feel guilty if they are involved in ministries of economic development among the poor, medical relief, educational or justice causes, because they think that the real task of a missionary must be evangelism and conversion. This, however, is an unnatural separation of the physical and spiritual aspects of salvation. The Jewish concept of salvation was never so dualistic as the Western church has transformed it, and the Biblical understanding of salvation is a very holistic approach, including both spiritual and physical changes.

A traditional evangelistic approach may be successful in bringing in large numbers, but it may hinder the subsequent spiritual formation of the new believers by failing to adequately demonstrate the strong connection of entrance in the Kingdom of God with real life--everyday issues like justice, peace and economics. While we traditionally teach new converts that they must amend their ways, we normally focus on the leaving of obvious sins such as lying, drunkenness and sexual immorality, and the taking on of activities such as reading the Bible, prayer and church attendance. However, many Christians can be in the church for years before ever being taught the radical concepts of agape love and the upside-down nature of relationships within the Kingdom of God.

For example, a traditional evangelistic approach consists of an intellectual appeal to the sinner, pointing out that God is pure and holy and cannot tolerate the presence of sin. We then proceed to convince the prospect that he or she is a sinner, underlining the fact that no one is innocent before God. Having convinced the person of their personal guilt before God, we proceed to explain God's answer to the problem by sending His son, Jesus Christ, into the world to take our sin upon himself and pay the price of death. At this point we explain the importance of faith in accepting the work of Christ on the cross and baptism into that experience to accept God's forgiveness of our sins (Acts 2:38). Next we affirm that the convert has entered God's kingdom, and we begin to teach him or her the new responsibilities and changes that will be required.

This approach is sound Biblically and doctrinally and through the ages, in various formats and presentations, has been used to bring millions of people into the Kingdom of God. However, often an intellectual assent to the truths presented in this evangelistic presentation does not produce, at least not as dramatically as would be desired, the radical changes in lifestyle that are a part of kingdom living. Not only that, but this approach is individualistic, often failing to bring about the conversions of whole people groups as in the book of Acts and throughout the history of the missionary movement. In a very individualistic, western society this method has more success than in other types of cultures.

Modern, western thought has often left out the community aspect of conversion, as well as the radical change of allegiance and authority that are needed to develop the type of spiritual formation of the church that we have seen in the early Jerusalem community. It appears that these early converts recognized on a practical level that their conversion was not simply a turning away from a life of sin, but a movement towards a new allegiance to Jesus Christ as Lord and an entrance into a new community.

The Two Kingdoms

In Uruguay, where I have been a missionary for the last ten years, we have been experimenting with another approach, emphasizing the existence of two different kingdoms. Most people live in the kingdom of darkness. The darkness is not necessarily a sign of rampant evil or horrible sins, although those things certainly exist and thrive in the darkness. Rather, the darkness speaks of deception and distortion. Those who live in the dark cannot see clearly and do not discern the true state of affairs. For this reason they are convinced that everything is fine. They are good people who fulfill their moral obligations and live peacefully with all. But they are deceived. They cannot see clearly in the dark. The kingdom of darkness is characterized by strife, disunity, loneliness and death.

The kingdom of light, however, is God's kingdom. Those of us who live in that kingdom are certainly not any better--at times we behave worse--than those in the kingdom of darkness. The major difference is that we now see things as they really are, and this gives us a totally new perspective on life. Entering this kingdom means turning one's life completely upside-down. The rich are the poor, the meek and lowly are the powerful, the servants are the lords and the children are the examples of maturity. In the Kingdom of God we love enemies, we give to those who ask, we go the second mile to help those who really do not deserve help, and we stubbornly refuse to let our diversity damage the unity of the community. Entering the Kingdom of God means more than simply accepting the forgiveness of sins or beginning to attend church services. It means changing allegiance to King Jesus and beginning to live life according to His teachings, which are radical indeed.

While it has been difficult to change the mentality of so many who have accepted the more individualistic approach to conversion, progress is being made in creating a sense of community with corporate responsibility. Poorer brothers and sisters are being taken care of, and unity is being fought for as we seek to allow diversity without allowing people to "go their own way." We are emphasizing and teaching the radical nature of Jesus' teaching, and the upside-down consequences of

life in the Kingdom of God. Spiritual formation, then, becomes not
something that takes place after conversion, but is rather an integral part
of the process.

How Can We Best Implement Spiritual Formation?

One of the most important questions for a church planting
missionary, however, is that to which we keep coming back. How do
we get this sort of unity and spiritual formation started? When a
missionary arrives on a field where there are no believers it is rather
difficult for one or two people to begin modeling community life. As
we seek to evangelize and bring people into the community of God,
how can we do so if the community does not yet exist?

Sensitivity to the Spirit

First of all, we must recognize that spiritual formation is
foremost the task of the Spirit. This is true as much in the beginning
stages of the conversion process as it is in the subsequent stages of
Christian maturity. I never cease to be amazed at the work of the Spirit
in convicting people of their need to submit to God. So often in spite
of our memorized and thoughtful evangelistic presentations we do not
see dramatic results. Yet, on other occasions when we feel that our
words and our arguments have been weak and inadequate, the Spirit
breaks through the barriers and hearts are broken and humbled before
God.

I will never forget a youth camp we organized several years
ago in a small town on the Uruguayan coast.   Three or four
missionaries, along with one Uruguayan minister rotated the preaching
responsibilities.   The missionaries, having more experience and
education brought intricate sermons, full of scriptural insight and poetic
illustrations, but when the decision time came the young people sat
calmly in their places. When Lauro, the Uruguayan minister preached,
he did so with little sophistication. His words were simple and his
thoughts were scrambled. His obvious nervousness only added to the
rambling nature of the message, yet even before he could finish and get
around to the invitation, one young man jumped up and said, "I want
to be a Christian." Another yelled out, "I do too," and still another and
another joined in. That evening we baptized five young people in the

name of Jesus Christ, not because of the power of cleverly constructed
sermons, but because the Spirit of God was at work.

The missionary must be very sensitive to the movement of the
Spirit of God, and must rely upon the work of the Spirit to call, convict
and bring people into His kingdom. The work of a missionary must be
bathed in prayer, and the church must be one committed to following
the Spirit's leading. The unity of the body of believers is bound up in
the work of the Spirit, and without the fruit of the Spirit it would be
impossible to achieve true community living. Just as the Jerusalem
church needed Pentecost before they could find unity in their diversity,
the mission church of today must seek the Spirit's work to create a true
sense of community.

Doing Away With Societal Ranking

This spiritual activity will undoubtedly bring about the feeling
of grace which gives a sense of security, which is absolutely essential
for true unity to take place. The Jerusalem church was not a true
homogeneous unit, since there were members from different parts of the
world speaking different languages. Nevertheless, the apostles exerted
much effort to make everyone feel that they were equal in the
community, and when problems later arose suggesting that certain
people were getting preferential treatment the leadership immediately
attacked the problem to underline the fact that by the grace of God all
members of the community were equal. This concept is one of the
fundamental differences between the kingdom of God and the kingdom
of darkness. In the world there is a highly organized system of ranks
and priorities depending upon roles, possessions, and education of a
person. In the kingdom of God, however, each member recognizes his
or her importance in the sight of God and His church.

This recognition is especially important when a missionary is
working among people of different social levels. Graciela is a young
lady who has had a very difficult life. Having grown up in poverty, she
raised her own children in a squatter settlement in Montevideo. When
we first met her she lived in a one room shack with no floor, no
electricity and no running water. Though she had the opportunity to
learn to read and write, she had not had a thorough education, and she
struggled to feel any self worth. When Graciela understood that Jesus
should be her King, and that He accepted her just as she is she entered

the kingdom of God and was immediately adopted by her new family. At first she felt uncomfortable entering our home, or sitting down to converse, but as she gradually came to realize that she was accepted as an equal in the church, she began to become more confident. She now actively participates in all of the activities of the church and is looked up to as a leader in the community. She not only experienced God's good grace, but is beginning to experience the grace of the outside community as well. Several people have commented on the change they have seen in her life, and many have entered the kingdom of God as a result of her testimony.

In order to make this grace visible it is necessary to strive constantly to erase any signs of stratification or rank within the congregation. We have struggled to make sure that every member actively participates in the worship services and other activities of the church, and we have made an effort to eliminate titles, positions and symbols of authority. Many of the wealthier members of the congregation resist the temptation to come to church with their most elegant clothing, and the poorer members strive to put on their best and in this manner we avoid dividing the congregation. A strong emphasis is made on the teaching of spiritual gifts and the fact that every member of the congregation is of vital importance to the ongoing growth and maturity of the church as a whole.

In this entire process the leadership of the congregation is a key element. The missionaries, together with the national leaders, must concentrate on spiritual formation through their verbal teaching, as well as by modeling through their life the kingdom principles necessary for true community life. The biblical principle of multiple leadership is crucial in developing a sense of community, since there will always be more than one person modeling the spiritual experience. This is a strong argument in favor of the missionary team as a means to plant churches, rather than an individual approach which tends to center around one person and his or her teaching.

Teaching Life Changing Principles

When we speak of verbal teaching we are not speaking only of basic doctrinal positions. Some missionaries feel that their task as a church planter is over if they have successfully evangelized and indoctrinated with the basics. This is true, only if we widen our understanding of the basics to recognize that a church is not a church unless it is a true, vital, living community.

Our verbal teaching must include instruction in the radical, life changing principles of life in the kingdom of God. We must go beyond the obvious teachings about honesty, purity and integrity, because most morally upright citizens in the kingdom of darkness already accept those as ideals towards which they need to strive. Our teaching must include the more difficult demands of our King, such as love for our enemies, economic justice and sacrificial self denial. Jesus says that we must give to all who ask. We must forgive even when the offender repeats the same offense time after time. We must not demand or defend our own rights but rather become the slaves of others. We must not even seek to preserve our own lives but rather offer ourselves as living sacrifices willing to die if that be necessary for the benefit of our brothers and sisters.

My experience has been that these concepts are extremely difficult to teach in the church; they are foreign to life as we know it. Even though we have moved from the kingdom of darkness into the kingdom of light, we continue to function using the thought processes and patterns of the kingdom of darkness. Nevertheless, Jesus has taught that these principles are fundamental for life in his kingdom, and we must strive to understand, comprehend and teach them to the emerging church. In Uruguay we have found it necessary to repeat constantly in sermons, lessons, and informal settings the radical nature of life as a true Christian.

Modeling Appropriate Lifestyles

Verbal teaching alone will never accomplish the task. Leaders must also model the lifestyle they are advocating. Several years ago, when we began considering opening a day care center for the children of a slum area in Montevideo, we hesitated because of the fear that the poverty of the neighborhood would tempt the people to abuse the privileges. However, as we moved into the community, got to know the people, entered their homes and conversed with them, we found that they began to know us on a more intimate level as well. They comprehended our motives and desires and they responded to our efforts lending a hand and struggling to protect the center against abuse. Though there are always exceptions, we have found that in general the community has not abused the generosity of the program, but rather has respected the attitude of those who are making the day care available. The program has attracted many souls to the kingdom of God.

Making the Love of Christ Manifest

This leads us to the last principle for true spiritual formation, and that is that the love of Christ must be made manifest in practical actions. Doctrinal teaching in the church is important, but if the love of God is not made manifest through practical actions, true spiritual formation will never take place. In the Jerusalem community the believers sold their possessions and had all things in common, so as not to allow anyone to suffer need. In the same way a church that is being planted must learn to translate her faith into actions that demonstrate the radical nature of the love of God. Too often the church is so absorbed in maintaining its programs and activities that this personal touch is lost.

I remember many years ago when a house a couple of blocks away from the church burned to the ground. The ministers of the congregation were some of the first to offer their condolences. They prayed with the family and they encouraged them to place their faith in God during this difficult time, but nothing practical was done. Nevertheless, the local socialist party did not allow even a day to go by before they had arranged for food, clothing and temporary shelter for the victims. The minister's words and prayers for the family rang empty in the light of the church's failure to translate God's love into action.

We have seen that spiritual formation is as much a part of evangelism as is the gospel presentation. A church cannot be considered planted if true spiritual formation is not taking place, and this is manifested through a vital sense of community. The missionary must, from the beginning, emphasize the formation of true spirituality among all of the converts so that community life can begin to take shape. As this life in community becomes more and more active, the unbelieving community will be able to look at the church and see a living example of what God's power can do in the lives of ordinary people. As the congregation grows and matures spiritually in this way, more unbelievers will be converted beginning the cycle once again. The church will be characterized by its powerful testimony as to the lordship of Christ, its incredible unity in spite of diversity, its solid leadership, and its ability to translate its faith into practical actions. And, underlying all of this, the church will experience much grace from God.

4

THE CHURCH PARTICIPATING IN DEVELOPMENT

by Greg Johnson

During this time some prophets came down from Jerusalem to Antioch. One of them, named Agabus, stood up and through the Spirit predicted that a severe famine would spread over the entire Roman world. (This happened during the reign of Claudius). The disciples, each according to his ability, decided to provide help for the brothers living in Judea. This they did, sending their gift to the elders by Barnabas and Saul (Acts 11:27-30).

Introduction

Development today has come a long way from the relief found in the book of Acts. In fact, relief has been redefined out of development by some since it is largely a response to an acute situation where a group of people cannot adequately feed, shelter or care for themselves. *Relief* comes after the problem whereas *development* targets the causes of community problems and attempts to enable people to sustain themselves. The one reacts to a problem such as famine, flood, earthquake or other disaster, while the other tries to anticipate, plan and work toward long term goals of development which will allow a people to remain self sufficient, even through natural calamity. For example, why does a typhoon in Bangladesh leave the area devastated, requiring major assistance from donor nations, while a hurricane in Florida, although difficult, leaves no one starving? Bangladesh as a country is not developed to the point where it can fully sustain itself, whereas the United States is an advanced developed nation.

In Acts 11 we find the church involved in relief. A famine, prophesied by Agabus, did in fact hit Judea in 46-48 AD, during the time of Claudius, a thirteen year reign "marked by successive droughts and bad harvests" (Bruce 1972:268). In this case relief came from the church in Antioch to the church in Judea. At the same time, the city of Jerusalem was receiving large gifts of money and food from proselytes Helena, the queen mother, and Izates, her son, the king of Adiabene from beyond the Tigris (Ibid.).

Relief was not new to the church. Soon after Pentecost the church became involved with relief for her own members. In Acts 6 the Grecian Jews called to the attention of the Hebraic Jews that their widows were being overlooked in the daily distribution of food. Later, during the persistent Judean famine, Paul encouraged the Corinthian church to join in giving to the church there. He explained to the Corinthian Christians how freely the Macedonians had given and, through their giving, had grown spiritually. These verses are instrumental in understanding Paul's ultimate goal through giving:

> I am not commanding you, but I want to test the sincerity of your love by comparing it with the earnestness of others. For you know the grace of our Lord Jesus Christ, that though he was rich, yet for your sakes he became poor, so that you through his poverty might become rich (2 Co 8:8-9).

Relief provided by the church brings twofold fruit. First, the givers grow spiritually. Paul was keenly aware of the spiritual dimension of giving, something that cannot be experienced until one has given freely. Secondly, relief directly assists fellow Christians who are having difficulty feeding themselves.

Throughout history the church has continued to generously take care of her own poor and widows. The church has also expanded to the point that there are now many church based relief and development agencies working all over the world. Tetsunao Yamamori, President of Food for the Hungry, has expounded the symbiotic approach to ministry, involving both social action and evangelism. The two, although separate, are integrated in the church's total responsibilities. Yamamori defines the "four R's of evangelical relief and development" which include *relief, recovery, redevelopment,* and *reconciliation*

(1987:132). Obviously not all four are required in all situations. Relief is temporary and should run the course of recovery and redevelopment as outlined by Yamamori. There will always be a dynamic tension between social action (the first three "R's") and evangelism, due to the limits of time and resources.

In 1983-85 the Maasai of Kenya were hit by the usual 10-12 year cycle of drought and famine. The Christian Missionary Fellowship team there was involved first in relief, then recovery. At first, Maasai families sold livestock and utilized traditional social systems to meet their food needs. As the drought continued and the livestock began to die, people ate some of the dying animals and sold the hides. Finally the drought persisted until the animals were so malnourished that hundreds died and there was a glut on hides; no one was able to help others or feed themselves.

Our program of food for work was supplied by the United States government through the agency Food for the Hungry. In my work area, the church took over the total responsibility for the entire project and divided the area into four distribution points. Church leaders led the communities out to various work projects, distributed the food and recorded each bag of maize meal given.

In moving from relief to recovery, a list was made of all families left totally destitute because of the drought. Each family was then restocked and put back on its feet as pastoralists once again. Seeing the renewed dignity of people driving home a small herd of sheep and goats greatly enhanced the Gospel as it was being proclaimed throughout the drought.

The church will always be involved in relief as in the book of Acts or in Maasai land, but development helps get a community or country further along so that when the natural disasters do come, the people are not totally devastated. For this reason I would like to focus more on development than on relief.

The Moral Imperative for Development

Due to the variety of both secular and Christian development missionaries need to consider the basis for development. Once the foundation is established for why missionaries or PVO's (Private Voluntary Organizations) do development, then the *how* can be explored. On what moral basis is Christian development different from that of the secularist? The morality for development among secularists is evident in their watchwords: people oriented; empowering the poor; genuine equality; distribution; self-reliance; sustainable growth; local participation, and self-determination.   Real development can only emerge when people are participators, not just executors of policy, programs or goals (O'Gorman 1978:8).

The Christian can agree with this moral position of secular development in so far as it goes. However, for Christians such a moral platform for intervention does not go far enough. The secular view of development is humanistic and not redemptive. Our differences begin with a Christian view of God, man and culture.

Created beings are made in the image of God and so Christians see culture as a gift of God. This view allows for the broad scope by which people worship, praise, exalt and express their adoration to God in so many varied ways.

Ultimately, God is in control--He created, He has moved throughout history, and even now He is reconciling people to Himself. This clearly puts the morality by which the Christian does development in a different light.   Our message and our Commission is both redemptive and inclusive. Therefore we can accept the secular platform for moral development, but for us as Christians, there is the larger goal of Kingdom both now and future.

This is not to say that Christian development is a deterministic or evangelistic ploy, but rather is motivated by our position in Christ. Christian development is performed out of Godly compassion, genuine Godly love and concern for the poor and suffering. We expect the growth of the Kingdom.   We do not have to apologize for our evangelistic approach.   Whereas secular developers see only this physical world, we see the world's poor and needy in larger spiritual dimensions.

Christian development goes far beyond the secularist morality when one considers what evangelism does for a community. Once alienated from God, the world's peoples become heirs through Christ (Eph 2:11-18). If Christians of the various world cultures are heirs, then a family of God has emerged thus fulfilling God's promise to Abraham (Gen 15:1-6; Gal 3:6-9). National boundaries are artificial and manmade as are the hostilities at work between nations.

It is important to note that for the Christian, evangelism is development. Evangelism is social change at the most rudimentary level, change from within the mind and heart of the individual moving out to family and community. As such, it is development. If we are one as Paul clearly states (Gal 3:26-29), then the Christian sent into the world by the Commission has a moral imperative for development, both in evangelism and in concern for physical suffering. Jesus' prayer was not to take the disciples out of the world but for protection from the evil one as He sent them into the world (Jn 17:15-18). The same mandate for relief inspired the disciples as they sent donations to the brothers and sisters in Judea because of the famine (Acts 11:27-30).

Development is difficult, time consuming and frustrating. In order to accept the responsibility for doing development, one must work through the *why*, thereby providing direction for development. It is not enough to say, "The people need help," or "The government demands assistance." As Christians, we must have a clear understanding of the morality by which we do development or we end up with little more than unfocused interventions with no clear direction. With a baseline commitment to the Kingdom, we can center our social action to strengthen and support local communities and the growth of the church. By having a clear moral basis for development, we can evaluate and determine the nature and type of projects we would be willing to undertake.

Historical Background of Development

Development experienced explosive growth in the post World War II era. A strong feeling emerged from the West that world poverty could be eradicated within a few short years. There was a naively positive idea that development was the "cure-all" for the world's problems and, with aid from the West, under- developed nations could soon enjoy prosperity and peace.

The predominant paradigm for development came to be modernization. This highly paternal model stemmed from the belief that "we" (the West) have it, and "they" (the under- developed nations) need it! Naturally leaders from these nations--many who had been trained in the West--gladly accepted foreign aid for industrialization, agriculture and health services. Also, many leaders embraced the modernized model for development of their rural areas to help underwrite their own national interests.

One needs to bear in mind that development has many different forms. For example, providing roads, electricity and water systems are larger governmental concerns. These forms of development are broader than single community development. Such development is macro, usually tied to the international scene and not generally within the scope of missionary development. Developers have been discouraged at the abuse, corruption and failure in macro projects.

Foreign aid is not without strings attached, because international development by donor nations is often politically motivated. In the past foreign aid has been used as ammunition in the ideological battle between communism and capitalism. Currently, Western donors are withholding aid to countries that are politically repressive and not moving toward multi-party structures. An official for USAID told a class I attended that when one country in Africa was not doing as the US desired, a project a day was halted until an agreement was reached.

Donor nations are not alone in using development to expand political influence. One should also look at the political ambitions and goals of the host country as the local political elites manipulate foreign aid to establish their own power, dominance and income. International development tends to be not only political but also top-down, with little or no regard for local peoples or their culture. Far too often, one finds the local communities with whom we work ultimately little more than pawns manipulated by the larger systems of national and international interests.

Rather than the positive effect of development that was predicted in the late 1940s and 50s, critics claim that the total effect of Western interventions on traditional societies has been under-development.

> Fiercely independent peoples who thrived for thousands of years in the world's harshest conditions now huddle in ragged bands by boreholes wells, waiting for food trucks. Blame is laid on nature, which persists, year after year, in following its fixed patterns. But man is responsible. We sought to improve on nature in Africa, and we failed disastrously. Rather than repairing damage already done, we are racing full tilt to commit the same errors on an even grander scale. We will not escape the price (Rosenblum and Williamson 1987:2).

Instead of the eradication of poverty, the gap between the rich and poor has grown, even though the GNP is up in some developing nations. The focus on GNP and industrialization is geared only toward national interests; rural communities are seen only in light of how they can be used to support national goals. Specific community needs for water, health or improved farming techniques are seldom considered, particularly in rural areas.

Living in such a complex geopolitical world causes one to question development, where much has failed, causing under-development and, in fact, greater suffering. Political realities can make even Christian development motivated out of compassion difficult to accomplish. Many involved in development have become cynical and skeptical. Case studies reveal few successes; in fact most projects require continual propping up by donors.

Common Problems in Development

Why has development sponsored by the international community and the church shown so few successes? Many books have been written on this subject, yet three key reasons for project failures should be mentioned.

A Faulty Assumption

First, both international and church development have often failed because of the faulty assumption that development is good and will succeed, leading to positive results. Development as such is not necessarily either good or bad; it can be good or bad or both. For example, in a class with Maasai church leaders I asked if schools were good, bad, or both good and bad. It was interesting to hear every single elder say schools were only good. Yet when we listed both the positive and negative aspects schools bring to the community, there were as many negative dimensions as positive. The men were astounded; they had never considered the down side to schools. On the positive side, it was noted that schools prepare people for jobs in a changing world, they bring awareness to the community, and they equip people to become part of national structures. But on the other hand, schools pull people away from community into individualism and materialism; traditional values are shunned. Although schools are important for communities to become part of a nation, there is also a downside to schools which many developers have not recognized, nor did that particular group of Maasai.

Insufficient Understanding

Secondly, projects have frequently been undertaken without sufficient understanding of local culture and values. Development without local participation, without any real regard for local culture, is known as "blueprint" or top down development. All cultures, societies, and countries are changing, and development is part of changing societies and countries. However, development can only be successful if the local values and needs are well defined and understood.

The Macro/Micro Chasm

Finally, the macro/micro chasm is a case in which the right hand does not know what the left hand is doing. Macro development tends to be top down, ultimately doing very little for rural conditions. Much of the church's development is so micro that it deals with the immediate needs of a local community but does not anticipate or link with the national. Communities are tied to national structures which have their own agendas for politics and development. Sometimes the national agenda is in conflict with a local community; therefore developers must seek to minimize conflict by a good flow of information and use of government channels into the local communities.

All countries will have some system for development. Missionaries need to identify the appropriate systems and work within them. Good communication and working through government channels reduces misunderstanding, fear and mistrust. To illustrate, there are many areas of Maasai land that need medical assistance. Yet, one church built a clinic where the Kenya government already had one. I know of several cases in which people went to the government clinic and received an injection, then went immediately to the church clinic and received another injection which caused the patients to go into shock from overdose.

Is Development Worth It?

Many people, both in development work and in the church, are asking this question. Consider the widespread use of boreholes in the fragile ecologies of East and West Africa and the Kalahari desert. Water projects have destroyed many areas by providing water when the people should have migrated as in the past. Overgrazing has now depleted so much pasture that pastoralists have forever lost much of their precious grazing land to desert.

Even in natural calamity the abuse of power and corruption have made relief difficult and frustrating. In the face of hunger, President Mohamed Khouna Haidalla, past president of Mauritania (since overthrown), was feeding his camels US aid donated flour. Mort Rosenblum related, "I asked how I could confirm it. Simple, he said, go kick open a camel turd. Before I got around to it, I met one of the truckers who was hired to hijack food for officials" (Rosenblum and Williamson 1987:59).

The case studies can go on and on leaving Western donors and workers with a sense of despair, questioning whether development can be achieved at all. No longer do developers simply feel the false optimism of assured success because of new technologies, hard work and new methods. Reality has shown otherwise, forcing people to look closer at cultural and political spheres. Unfortunately, church sponsored development, like secular development, has had a poor success rate.

Overall, missionaries are in a good position to follow through on our ideological morality for development and to succeed. Missionaries live within communities, learning the language and culture. We hear, feel and experience the joys and sufferings of those around us. I can well remember the height of our 1983-85 drought in Kenya when those Maasai who share the name of Christ and co-labored with me in the growth of His Kingdom had a mere fraction of the food I had available to me. Such situations prick our sensibilities and can make good food look and even taste bad. Being within communities, as we gain command of the language and culture and the confidence of the people, we can plan and work through the local communities in such a way as to meet their needs with them. Considering the many forms of development brought to the developing world today, Christian development based on a biblical view of people, God and Kingdom should have the greatest impact and the highest success rate.

Understanding that we have a moral responsibility for development leads us to ask, "How do we do development?" What model best suits us? Missionaries have the opportunity to become involved in full participatory development in which the people themselves plan and work toward improvement as they see fit. The presence of missionaries and the growth of the church should bring an awakening to the community, whether rural or urban. Although our message is not usually political, the total impact of living and serving the needs of a community ought to help them more broadly see the world, their government and what they can expect from government.

The "How" of Development...Participatory Development

With this background in mind, participatory development can be defined as a "process whereby people learn to take charge of their own lives and solve their own problems" (Bunch 1982:28). In other words, "where people are gaining the self-confidence, motivation, character traits, and knowledge needed to tackle and solve the problems they have by actually solving and tackling those problems," people are participating in their own development (Bunch 1982:28). This is not to say that an outsider with a suggestion or idea is not of value. Change is a process that all communities are experiencing and people will likely participate when they feel that the benefits will outweigh the costs of capital, time or effort required. As missionary change agents we have the opportunity to bring ideas, suggestions and opportunities to local communities for participatory development.

Programs must do something for people or they will not be successful, but participation must avoid what Bunch calls the "paternalism of the give-away" or the "paternalism of doing things for people" (1982:20-21). The opposite of such paternalism is participation with the community and linking the community to the needed agencies, technologies and government structures.

Positive and Negative Factors in Participatory Development

Regardless of the theoretical model used, no development is without problems. Along with the positive dimensions of participatory development, there are also problems that need to be recognized and addressed.

Positive Factors in Participation

Participatory development:
a) is project oriented or micro specific, which allows concentration on a single problem or need.

b) is neither top-down nor trickle-down.

c) is based on better information because it is local information.

d) is decentralized, allowing for larger involvement without central authority.

e) is not management intensive.

f) desires to expand local resources, technologies and skills.

g) involves the community so that it will more likely work to maintain the project after completion.

Negative Factors in Participation

a) Participatory development projects take longer to design and implement.

b) Management is often so loose that lines of communication and authority get confusing.

c) Coordination and timing of efforts can become protracted and drawn out.

d) What happens when there is conflict of interests among the participants. Sometimes communal goals run contrary to individual goals.

e) There is the problem of "free-riders," that is, those who benefit yet contribute nothing.

f) If the project is too local it will have trouble surviving
    over a longer period of time, because it does not coordinate
    with larger regional and national goals.

g) Bottom-up development often does not account for organizing
    costs.

h) Capital costs raised locally seldom meet ongoing operating
    costs.

According to Hyden one of the problems with participatory development is that it tends to be too ideological and difficult to operationalize. He feels one can quibble with the very word itself, "participation;" how much is there in a project?

For example, every project has at least six stages. *Initiator.* There are those who have initiated the project. How much, if any, local participation is there? Many projects originate at the local level so participation exists from the outset. Missionaries may bring ideas for development; however, as outsiders we should be very careful not to push our suggestions. If the community perceives that a project has merit, it will work toward implementation.

Sponsorship and ownership. Is it clear who owns the project? Here, too, participation can easily be built in if the missionary is careful to work with the local people.

Design. At the very least, stated felt needs and proposals for resolution can come from the local community, but if the project is very technical, then participation is limited, requiring specialized skills. To illustrate, the Maasai in one location was to irrigate. To do so, the river has to be raised through a dam so that the water can be brought by gravity to the garden plots. The design of such a project is technologically out of the hands of the local Maasai, which is alright so long as they can maintain the project.

Decision making. The decision making process includes the initial decision to go ahead with the project as well as all decisions throughout the project. The tendency is for the missionary to make these decisions because it is expedient.

Project execution. Here people can obviously become involved in a variety of ways--labor, technology and funding.

Evaluation. Who does it? When is it done? How is evaluation incorporated into project change to keep the beneficiaries foremost?

So, for each part of a project, inputs are required, which should allow for participation at various levels.

For all the delays, potential problems and frustration in participatory development, it is still by far the better model than the modernization paradigm of the past or the top-down "blueprint" approach. This model allows people to share in their own destiny, to help coordinate efforts based on their felt needs and, through participation, the project's chances of success are greater. It is true that parts of some projects may be more participatory than others but if the ideas, design, implementation and evaluation include the local community, then the project has more likelihood of success. Strategies properly designed can minimize conflict, encourage cooperation, provide information to the participants, and keep communication open.

Strategies for Participatory Development

Incentives

At the heart of participatory development is the assumption that people are rational. Participation is an "investment" based on the anticipated returns (Bryant and White 1984:9). As outsiders we need to bear in mind the risk factor for the community. For us, there is no risk, but for a farmer or herder or poor urban dweller, the project may be asking too much: what if the project should fail? What will they eat next season? An intervention will be more readily entered into by a community if the venture is not perceived as too economically risky.

People do have a community consciousness and will work for community goals when the community goals also benefit the participating individuals. People will spend more of their time, effort and resources based on expected returns. The incentives that will bring community participation must be clearly identified by the people before a project can be designed.

Goal Setting

The community needs to discuss their priorities and set goals. Exactly what participation is or means must be defined and understood by all involved in the project: the donors, the local people, and the government. Next, all ideas, expectations and goals of the project must be reviewed by the participants before the project is actually designed. Exactly what is wanted and expected out of the project? Who are the intended beneficiaries and how will they benefit?

I have had an unpleasant experience because I thought all the expectations had been defined but later learned that no real consensus existed. One group of Maasai came to me and asked for help in getting a diesel powered mill for grinding maize. The project was initiated by local women who identified their goal as having their maize ground locally rather than having to take it some forty-four kilometers round trip for grinding. It was not until after the funding came through and the mill set up that I learned the women wanted to make profit off the mill and could not agree on how the profit should be divided--for individuals or for the whole group.

The mill sat idle for several months while the women argued. Even now, as the mill is running, there is no agreement on how it will be maintained or the profits shared. Consequently, it is only a matter of time until the project will fail for lack of unified goals and expectations of what the mill will do for the women. It is important that the community arrive at a sense of unity and solidarity. All hidden agendas must be brought out in the discussions since each person may come to the project with an idea of what the project will do for them. Only when project goals are clearly understood and agreed upon by all involved can the project be successfully designed.

Design

The beginning of success or failure is in the project design. Projects should be kept fairly small and simple. Even the larger international donor agencies are beginning to see that greater success comes through smaller, specific, task-directed projects. This allows the community to participate yet does not overwhelm them. Not all problems need to be tackled at once. Integrated projects can be added in time as local perceived felt needs are clarified. Technologies and resources need to heighten local expertise without going so far that the community is dependent on resources and technologies that may not be available to them.

A second essential to project design is the formulation of a local committee with advocates from the community to the community. This means that there is a strong current of communication and flow of information. When information is flowing suspicions of the project's motives are dispelled. Failure to understand how relationships are formed, information is shared, or decisions are made within a community is the reason so much top-down development is flawed. Being missionaries does not exempt us from being top-down. It is the free flow of information from a committee set by the local people that enables us as missionaries to know the way in which people perceive benefits and choose to become involved. In this way, the committee is able to build on the interests and genuine needs of the local people so participation can be seen as a benefit and not merely a cost.

Local resources, which include local expertise, cash, land, labor, tools and technologies, can then be invested into the project. The involvement of local resources gives the project a much better chance of long-term success. It is also important that information continue to be free flowing throughout the life of the project in order to allow the project to adapt and change as circumstances require.

Local Leadership and Ownership

In participatory development the training of local leaders is essential. Local administration exists everywhere; the goal is to work through the committee, enhancing the local leadership's abilities and training them to coordinate the project, to think creatively and to protect the project from being commandeered by elites. This allows local leadership to mature and to develop a sense of confidence and pride in their achievements.

Setting up a committee is difficult and time consuming, particularly in rural areas. Without local leadership, however, the project is destined to fail. Decisions do take longer but as the committee learns to function properly, it can assist in conflict resolution among the project members and keep one individual from becoming a free-rider or using the project for personal benefit. The committee also provides the format for linking the project with larger regional and district authorities.

There is another critical factor to a successful committee. The community must elect the members for themselves and they must trust the committee to function. My unhappy experience with the maize mill was further complicated because the women did not trust each other enough to elect a committee. They trusted me, expecting that I would run the mill for them and give them all of the profits. Since the mill belongs to the women's group, I have refused to make the mill my responsibility beyond helping them to get it set up. I told them they needed to elect a committee that I could train to watch over the mill, keep books, and save some money for maintenance and repairs. Finally, a recipe for disaster developed; with the women unable to agree, the men finally chose a committee of women to oversee the mill and only one member of this committee has shown any interest at all! Lack of trust has immobilized the project and although the mill project was begun at their initiative, there is nothing I can do until the community elects a committee and empowers them to function. Any project must be designed so that the community can consider the options and be empowered to make decisions.

Timing

Timing is also a crucial factor to the success of a project. For example, in areas where roads are very bad, a community may pull together and build a road in order to enable vehicles to bring in supplies. In the Samburu District of Kenya, one community was willing to build a road if our mission would place a missionary family in the area. The community was willing to expend the effort knowing that through a missionary, various helps would come into the community. Since we did not place a family in the area, the timing was wrong and the road has not been built. It is the same for people living beside a beautiful stream. Unless the local people see the benefits to gardening, any irrigation scheme is premature.

Evaluation

Success is important and the earlier visible success occurs, the greater the enthusiasm and support for the project. It is much harder to develop enthusiasm towards interventions when people have experienced failure in the past. Failure, in fact, inoculates people against development and is thereby harmful. Although early success is important, a project must have long term benefits as well. In order to determine growth, some form of evaluation must be in place. This usually requires measurements, data collection and record keeping. The data should be kept minimal, simple and appropriate. Through evaluation people will be able to know if they are getting what was predicted or anticipated.

Linking Participatory Development

The three spheres in participatory development which need to be linked are the *private* sector, the *government* sector, and the *voluntary* sector, such as missions or private voluntary organizations. These sectors can be pictured as three individual circles that at points intersect with each other. Each sector has its own set of goals, yet all need to be in coordination so that the project will be in sync with community, regional and national aims.

The private sector participants are looking for benefit, usually some sort of material or economic gain or perhaps prestige. The government sector is concerned with the state's control, integrated national development, and taxes. The voluntary sector groups have humanitarian and spiritual concerns, a desire to assist people in meeting their physical and spiritual needs.

There will be times when two of the sectors work closely together, such as the local community and a private voluntary organization, but the core to successful development is the linking of all three. Seeing how the three spheres work together toward strong participatory development will be helpful.

Private Participants and Local Institutions

Every culture has local institutions in place and strengthening these will enhance a project's chances of success. New institutions should be put in place only when absolutely necessary. According to Uphoff, some of the local institutions likely to be found are: 1) local leadership, 2) private enterprise, 3) member organizations such as self-help groups, user groups, groups pooling resources such as labor, tools or capital, and 4) use-management which directs people and households "according to community norms and personal understandings of the limits and possibilities of resource exploitation" (1986:22).

Through identifying local institutions and energizing them, missionaries can secure information reflective of genuine felt needs, can work through a truly representative committee, and can help the community link with the government. This, then, is true community-based development.

Government Institutions

In any country where one is a guest, one way to jeopardize one's relationship with the government is to work without the proper district authorities knowing what projects are being undertaken. Since cultures are surrounded by government authority, all governments will exercise the right to know what kinds of development are going on and to fit local development into their national goals. Difficulties can be reduced by notifying authorities and working through proper channels.

The government has many resources for development such as extension programs, experimental stations, training seminars, community programs, farming, veterinary, and water specialists, and sometimes funds which can be tapped for information or assistance. Central authority has its own goals and they do not always harmonize with the local community's, but there is value in central authority to maintain law and order. Almost any form of participatory development can fit under a government's umbrella. I have used various government specialists in water, veterinary and health fields at no cost except for transport. Potential alienation, fear and distrust can be diffused by keeping government officials informed on what is happening and who is involved.

Voluntary Organizations

By living in the communities we seek to reach with the Gospel, and learning the language and culture of those whom we are called to serve, we, as missionaries have the unique opportunity to see real participatory development happen. We know the leaders, their personalities, their strengths and weaknesses. We should be a stimulus, in sharing ideas and helping people work through their problems to develop goals that are manageable. More than most we should be able to help communities set up local committees and projects that keep the intended beneficiaries to the fore, allowing local initiative to emerge and be strengthened.

Missionaries disciple leaders in programs all over the world; we more than most should be able to encourage and build confidence with local administration and leadership. We know the local resources, capital, land, labor, technologies and expertise. We should be able to link the local people to the outside world and to the government. We do have a role to play in development. Our role may at times be shared with governments or secularists, but we are spurred on by a much higher, nobler sense of global family that can be found only in our Lord and His commission that we carry to the world.

As Christians we have a moral imperative for development and the alleviation of suffering. Calling it symbiotic ministry, community development or self-help, we do have a role in the communities that we seek to serve. We bear a message that liberates from the bondage of sin and transforms misery into joyful communion with God. We have the opportunity to do development through love in such a way that will leave communities more self-reliant and able to cope with national interests, and yet maintain their own dignity.

> Go to the people
> Live among them
> Learn from them
> Love them
> Serve them
> Plan with them
> Start with what they know
> Build on what they have.
>
> (Chinese Wisdom Saying)

5

PERSECUTION THEN AND NOW

by David and Sheela Lall

It was about this time that King Herod arrested some who belonged to the church, intending to persecute them. He had James, the brother of John, put to death with the sword. When he saw that this pleased the Jews, he proceeded to seize Peter also. This happened during the Feast of Unleavened Bread. After arresting him, he put him in prison, handing him over to be guarded by four squads of four soldiers each. Herod intended to bring him out for public trial after the Passover. So Peter was kept in prison, but the church was earnestly praying to God for him (Acts 12:1-5).

"Rejoice in the Lord always, and again I say rejoice!" (Phil 4:4). What an offbeat opening note to an article on persecution--talking about everlasting joy. Yes, the secret of inner joy comes to us and fills us with a glowing, bubbling real joy when we are in Christ. It is never affected by the physical and financial status of our existence. Circumstances and conditions may weaken our body but they can never touch our inner soul, and we learn to understand that when we are in Christ He leads our lives for His eternal glory.

As second generation missionaries to India, we can well identify with persecution which might aptly be called the barometer of any missionary's work. Our father often said, "Don't you ever be worried when persecuted, worry only if you are not persecuted because then it means even Satan is not considering your efforts for the Lord worthy enough for his Satanic trials through which God is bound to show His miraculous victory causing triumphant gain of more people for His Kingdom."

A real Christian is one who identifies with Christ and therefore must suffer His reproach. Jesus said, "All men will hate you because of me..." (Mt 10:22). He also stated, "If the world hates you, keep in mind that it hated me first. ... If they persecuted me, they will persecute you also" (Jn 15:18,20). Suffering for Christ is the hallmark of a real Christian.

India is a land of religious pluralism. The majority religious group is the Hindu community in this nation of 88 million people. Christians make up only about 2.5% of the population. Despite the secular ideologies in post-colonial India, there are instances of organized persecution inflicted on the body of Christ by the majority Hindu religious group.

There is no doubt that the power of the majority has crept into the religious, political and cultural life of the nation. The Hindus are well aware of their strength as the single largest group and they could well be termed "fanatics." Some Hindus continue to advocate the naive idea of Hindu nationhood espoused by V. D. Savarkar and Golwakar in 1939. This revivalistic and exclusivistic movement differs from the more humanistic vision of Mahatma Ghandi. Jawahar Lall Nehru strongly advocated the idea of unity in adversity as the main feature of the India's historical reality. His idea is predominantly a Hindu concept, but is yet to be realized in its true sense.

The problem in India is one of enormous complexity of class, creed, ethnic and minority groups striving for social justice. This justice can only be achieved on the basis of equality, understanding and love as demonstrated by Jesus Christ.

Followers of Jesus Christ are called upon to serve humanity without thought of class or ethnic distinction. Hindu fanatics misinterpret the attitude of Christian missionaries and their concept of service as attempts to proselytize by offering bribes and incentives to people. Christians in India are also looked upon as the followers of an alien religion preached by the British rulers who enslaved India for nearly four hundred years.

This suspicious attitude continues even in present day India despite the religious freedom guaranteed in the constitution. If a true seeker receives a copy of the Bible it is considered as a bribe to lead him or her to convert to the Christian faith. Such an allegation is not only baseless but also a mischievous lie which is used to drag Christians to court and create problems for their work. False propaganda is carried out against Christians with the intention of causing mental torture and persecution.

Persecution of Early Christians

In Acts chapter 12 we read of persecution leveled at Christians because of their faith. Historical sources other than the Bible tell us that the Herod of this passage is Herod Agrippa I, whose grandfather was Herod the Great. The younger Herod was born in 11 A.D. and became the ruler of Judea in 41 A.D. Herod Agrippa was a popular ruler with the Jewish people, and he studiously sought to cultivate their favor.

When Herod learned that the Jews were antagonistic towards the apostles, he moved quickly to have some of them arrested. James, the son of Zebedee, was the first victim, and he met his death with the sword--most likely he was beheaded. The intention of this officially sanctioned persecution was the physical, mental and social humiliation and breaking of a person to his or her lowest possible ebb.

The Biblical word used for the persecution initiated by Herod against the Christian community is *kakosai*. While the particular usage in Acts 12:1 is not used elsewhere in Scripture, we know that the meaning of the term is to hurt, to maltreat, to afflict, or to cause bodily injury (Kittel 1971:484).

The favor of the Jewish people led Herod to arrest Peter. Cassidy writes that "Herod had acted on his own initiative in proceeding against James. However, the positive response that he received from "the Jews" provided him with encouragement and reinforcement for moving in a similar fashion against Peter" (1987:19). Peter was arrested at the beginning of season of unleavened bread. He was put into jail under heavy guard to insure that he would not escape or be set free by the Christians. Following the Passover, Herod intended to have Peter brought forth from prison, tried and executed.

Only those who were true disciples of Christ were subjected to Herod's persecution. Herod had to resort to the ruse of some law to "legally" persecute the Christians. The apostles and the early church took notice. In the face of discouragement, however, we must also note the following. The church was constantly in an attitude of prayer. Believers earnestly sought God's help and guidance during this time of difficulty. The prayers of the righteous were such that Peter was about to miraculously escape prison.

The words, "Fear not for I am with you always," seem to come alive from the story of the miraculous escape of Peter from the Roman prison--from the chains of power, from the mental and physical tension and pain, from the bondage of suffering and shame. It was a victorious escape, witnessing to a power beyond the ability of the Apostles. Do not those trying to spread the Gospel throughout the world today go through similar situations?

What is Persecution?

We would like to define persecution as *hurting or harassing people for their principles and beliefs.* Like a rainbow, persecution has many hues and shades. Even though sometimes wrapped in ugliness and pain, it can turn out to be a beautiful fulfillment of God's covenant with His people. The beauty of the outcome can cover the scars and show to the world the wonderful miraculous love of a caring Father.

The forms of persecution can vary from mental to physical torture or be in the form of a social boycott. We may consider ourselves blessed that we are not burned alive or shot down for the public declaration of our faith and we can thank God for our lives. History is a witness to many forms of persecution. Some of the experiences of those persecuted are not only a source of inspiration and encouragement to us in our times of trial, but also strengthen our everlasting bond with Christ expressed in faith, love and joyous victory. Paul's words are especially meaningful:

> But he said to me, 'My grace is sufficient for you, for
> my power is made perfect in weakness.' Therefore I
> will boast all the more gladly about my weaknesses,
> so that Christ's power may rest on me. That is why,
> for Christ's sake, I delight in weakness, in insults, in
> hardships, in persecutions, in difficulties. For when
> I am weak, then I am strong (2 Co 12:9-10).

No matter how painful the experiences, persecution, defamation and death have added to the number of believers throughout the world, hoisting the victorious flag of Christ with the motto of His last commission.

Persecution in India

Why then in India are Christians so few in number? There are only two reasons. First, only 52% of the people in India are literate, and second, 70% of the population still live in villages. These are god-fearing people. However, they face tremendous social problems such as untouchability and superstition. In addition, Hindu political parties based on communalism have gained an edge over secular-minded political parties. Invariably, the communal parties look upon the minority religious groups, such as Christians, as alien. Their feelings are intensified because of the false notion of Christianity being a Western religion propagated by the former British rulers.

The Hindu people have been attracted by the comfortable lifestyle of the West and have been quick to adopt the same lifestyle, but with scant regard for the religion that the rulers practiced. Instead of imbibing the values of Christianity, present day Indian society has sacrificed even their rich traditional morals and values in favor of an easy-going life. Corruption allows many to secure the extra money needed to meet the heavy demands of such a life. Moral decadence has resulted and people have come to accept corruption as a way of life. In contrast, when a believer leads a life of honesty and sacrifice, he or she has to face persecution in daily life.

Our Story

Persecution in India can be traced back several generations. The experiences of our own family are typical of what has happened to many others. Yet it is not just the cry of the past but a present reality as the fires of persecution are still very much in evidence.

Around the turn of the century in the suburb of Jabalpur (a major city in the central part of India) lived a high-class Hindu family. In that household the women were educated--something quite unusual in those days. When some missionaries heard about this, they persuaded the head of the family to allow the women to come and teach in their school and help educate the females in the area. It was agreed that the missionaries would send a horse-drawn carriage for the transportation of the women who would educate the girls and the ladies around the area as part of their social and patriotic responsibility.

While teaching in the mission school, these women came to know about Christ, the only true Lord and Savior. They desired to become Christians. When the men of the family heard about it, they were furious. In a society where men dominated and where an orthodox religious system existed, this incident became an issue of prestige for the family. The decision of the women was unacceptable. Hence they decided to kill the women. In their minds, by becoming Christians the women were bringing shame and suffering to the family. But God had a specific plan for the future of these women. A well-wisher told them about the plot of their family, and they escaped in the night by walking seven miles through the jungle to reach the mission station.

The next morning, one male member of the family traced the women and his four year old son to the mission station. He tried to force them to return, but his efforts were in vain. He said to his wife, "You are dead to us anyway. We will have nothing to do with you, but give me my son back." Later he filed suit in a court of law, but he died of plague while the court case was still in process.

Naturally the mother had custody of the boy. But soon after this incident, she developed a high fever and died. The boy was an orphan at the age of four and lived with his aunt. He became a laughing stock--living proof, it was thought, of a curse fallen on his family because of his mother's acceptance of Christ. The boy's name was Samuel Prem Lall. He grew up in a mission school and later became manager of that very school and orphanage. He married and had three children: Vijay Lall, Stanley Lalit Lall and Ramola Lall Henry. All three of his children became Christian evangelists in India.

Vijay Lall, our father, was disillusioned with the existing system of the Christians and strove to make the body of Christ intelligible to seekers. Afraid and insecure, the church leaders chose to lose a disciple rather than to change their old ways of conducting church affairs. Vijay Lall began a crusade--single- handedly leading believers, writing books and teaching. He had to resign from his job as superintendent of twenty-three schools as the leaders were trying to create a hierarchy and he was opposed. He ended up with fourteen court cases lodged against him and his friends. His time and energy were consumed in clearing himself of the charges without compromising his beliefs and principles. He was persecuted by Christians, non-Christians, and government officials who viewed his new movement with fear and suspicion. Lall won all 14 court cases and by God's grace emerged victorious from the burning fire. He had the power to bear persecution.

Lall's work resulted in the formation of the Mid India Christian Mission which today includes Hindi and English schools, an eye hospital, a Bible college, a printing press, a media production and training center, and a benevolent program aimed at children, widows and the elderly. Other activities include starting new churches as well as encouraging existing congregations. All of these activities have been possible because of the vision, faith and determination of Vijay Lall. During his lifetime, he not only built buildings, he built people to carry on this God-oriented work.

Joy Despite Persecution

Every phase of the ministry has its own unique history. It is a story of victory through persecution. When the schools were first being established Bible lessons were taught. A powerful orthodox Hindu leader led a movement against the work. He tried his best to convince the parents of the students as well as the government officials that the students would eventually be forced to change their religion. He tried to close the schools, but the dedicated teaching staff worked hard to impart the best possible education to the children. The school achieved extremely high examination results. Noting the general conduct and discipline of the students, the Hindu leader came to the school and apologized, saying that his actions were based on biased and prejudiced thinking. He said that the teaching of Christ is good for the overall personality of a person. Now he wanted his own children to be admitted to the school!

Opposition also came when the eye hospital was established. As the patient's physical eyes were healed, their spiritual eyes could be opened to see the beauty of God again. Some leaders tried to mislead people by saying that they would be at the mercy of the hospital workers. If they did not accept Christ, they were told, they might be blinded for life. Fear, anger and suspicion among the patients resulted. But prayerfully the staff attended to the people's physical and spiritual needs. Many overcame their ailments and have had their vision restored. At the same time their hearts have been touched.

One leader who opposed the hospital had a massive heart attack. He needed oxygen at once and he was also advised by a local physician to go immediately to a nearby medical college and research center some 100 miles from the hospital for treatment. This took place in the middle of the night, and the eye hospital was the only place in the region where they could find oxygen and an ambulance. He was helped in his dilemma. The life of a person who sought to destroy the ministry was saved by people associated with the ministry. Since that time he is a changed man, always praising the work and attitude of those who helped him.

Another fanatical Hindu leader owns a newspaper agency. He needed major eye surgery. During his stay in the hospital we spent hours studying and talking together at his request. Now he has read the entire Bible and some other Christian literature. Recently he sent word that he would like to attend Bible college.

New Avenues of Ministry

When my family and I wanted to dedicate ourselves to full-time service for the Lord, people raised questions as to what an engineer with a Master's degree in psychology could do for the mission. But my family and I had a passion to use our talents for the Lord. We could foresee that a key to more effective world evangelism is through the use of hi-tech media. We could visualize the change it could bring to aimless, bored and frustrated young people. We could perceive the bleak future of broken families as the result of the low priority given to God in their lives. Such people are willing to do anything for the fulfillment of their desires. Unless and until they hear the Word of God loudly and clearly and go back to the Bible, they will not be drawn to God. This has become our burden and we have focused our attention on this specific need.

When people saw our ministry, some militant Hindu extremists accused us of being agents of the CIA as our financial help comes mainly from America. This accusation seems trivial, but it has been the cause of many problems. One of the major difficulties we faced was when we tried to build an audio-visual studio. At that time all the television and radio stations were owned by the government. There was pressure from all sides as we found ourselves in a tight situation with no possible solution--humanly speaking--in sight.

We knelt down and joined our hands in earnest prayer, seeking God's direction by lifting our hearts and eyes to Him, trusting Him for a miracle to guide us in our hour of trial. Suddenly a bright light filled the room and shone upon us. Empowered by the Spirit of God, we stepped forward to pay the price of faith and vision.

We began making numerous trips to our state capital and to our national capital. Every time we went to officials with hope and expectation, but our efforts were brutally crushed by an anti-Christian attitude. We continued to trust in God and waited patiently for His timely guidance with His words in mind: "Do not be afraid of what you are about to suffer. I tell you, the devil will put some of you in prison to test you, and you will suffer persecution for ten days. Be faithful, even to the point of death, and I will give you the crown of life" (Rev 2:10).

Now the very people who tried to uproot the idea of the mission are taking advantage of its various phases. The people who held public meetings at the center of the town against the work have understood that we do not just preach the love of Christ--we practice it in life. They are now friendly to us.

The government officials who tried to crush our efforts are gladly inviting us to register ourselves as their official producers for Christian programs on special occasions. Through top quality Christian films and the educational and short television films we have produced, we have gained credibility in their eyes. We have tried to satisfy physical and spiritual needs of people through the ministries of the mission.

None of this has been accomplished without persecution, but true to His word, we have felt God's presence even in times of trials and sufferings. We have drawn strength from the Lord's reassuring promise, "Be strong and courageous. Do not be afraid or terrified because of them, for the Lord your God goes with you; he will never leave you nor forsake you" (Deu 31:6).

One of our preachers, Mr. Soni, shared his life story. He came from a nice and well-to-do Hindu family. He was a brilliant student, but during his third year at Medical College became a drug addict. He was frustrated with his life. Medical treatment for his addiction was unsuccessful. He tried to commit suicide. But God helped him through a Christian friend who shared the Gospel with him and rescued him from the suicide attempt. He accepted Christ and was delivered from his drug addiction. But his family was not pleased--even though they knew that he had changed for the better and had been delivered from drugs.

He had to face severe persecution from his family who rejected him. Unable to endure the rejection, Mr. Soni left home and led a lonely life for seven years. Members of his family tried to follow him everywhere putting many trials and hurdles before him and testing his faith with many forms of persecution. He was handed over to the police on false charges. The police were bribed and punished him brutally in order to try to persuade him from following Christ. True friends came to his rescue like angels from God. A new chapter has begun in Mr. Soni's life. He is happily married and has three children. Now he is working full time for the Lord. He is committed to expending himself for the Lord's kingdom at all times. He often faces persecution and ends up in jail. However, now even the police have become friends with him because of his loving attitude. He is patiently serving the Master while rejoicing in victory with many new converts.

Conclusion

Christians should unite at the present time. The world is needy, as the following words from an unknown author reveal:

> Tonight the world is burning
> and I am dying too.
> But there is no death more certain,
> than death inside of you.
> Some men die of shrapnel,
> some go down in flames.
> But most men die inch by inch
> while playing little games.

Persecution inevitably follows those who belong to Christ and witness of their faith in Him. "For it has been granted to you on behalf of Christ not only to believe in him, but also to suffer for him..." (Phil 1:29). These words remind us that faith in Christ is filled with perils and persecution, but it is not without rewards. Paul, himself a prisoner for Christ, saw the connection between his persecution and the progress of the gospel in Roman halls of power. Because of that, he could rejoice and urge all persecuted Christians to do the same.

Let us prayerfully and humbly, but firmly and boldly, with joyful obedience to God, face the world of latter day Herods. Even if we are arrested because of our Christian faith and made to pay the price of discipleship by persecution, we may be able to witness the miracles and victory of Christ. The assurance of God will strengthen us to say, "For to me, to live is Christ and to die is gain" (Phil 1:21). May God bless us and help us to find the dynamic power available through persecution for world evangelism.

6

AFTER THEY HAD FASTED AND PRAYED

by Effie Giles

In the church at Antioch there were prophets and teachers: Barnabas, Simeon called Niger, Lucius of Cyrene, Manaen (who had been brought up with Herod the tetrarch) and Saul. While they were worshiping the Lord and fasting, the Holy Spirit said, "Set apart for me Barnabas and Saul for the work to which I have called them." So after they had fasted and prayed, they placed their hands on them and sent them off (Acts 13:1-5).

Pages from a Journal

"After fifteen and a half years, we're going back. What will we find? Some things we already know. At Yasow the houses are burned to the ground. At Haro the houses are stripped of everything movable and removable, leaving only shells of former mission residences. But the important thing is what has happened in the lives of the people. What will we find? Children who were five years old when we left are now twenty. Many of the old people have died and all (including us) have aged. A whole generation has grown up since we left. What has the Holy Spirit brought from seeds planted so long ago? The next few days will begin to tell the story..."

This excerpt was written in my journal on October 2, 1992 as we waited for the helicopter flight from Addis Ababa, taking us back to western Wollega, where Christian Missionary Fellowship missionaries had pioneered in bringing the gospel to the Oromo and Gumuz people in the 1960s and 1970s. When Marxism gained full control in 1977, all the missionaries in CMF had to withdraw, leaving a church of about four thousand baptized believers, scattered in small congregations all across the highlands and among the lowland Gumuz people.

We already had some clues as to what had happened in the intervening years. We had been able to maintain sketchy contact, through letters which made their way to Addis Ababa by traders who had travel passes to come in to buy goods. A Christian man from that area who had moved to Addis Ababa was a major contact in getting those letters to us, and in seeing that the letters we wrote eventually got to the believers in a discreet way. One of the letters which gave us great encouragement was from a graduate of Addis Ababa University, sent by the Marxist government to teach school in Gidda, a "county seat" village in the heart of the area where we had lived and worked. He wrote about his faith. He told of coming in contact with Afeta and Hiticha, two strong believers, Oromo farmers who though limited in their education, were testimonies to God's power at work. He wrote, "The seed that you sowed has not remained unfruitful. Actually, it has brought (forth in) a most surprising way."

In 1985, during the peak of the famine which engulfed Ethiopia, God opened the door for some of us to return to Ethiopia, seconded to an aid organization--Food for the Hungry--to work in famine relief. Though not allowed to return to the area where we had previously worked, we were able to reestablish contact with some of the Christians.

In 1988 Ray, my husband, came to Addis Ababa to meet with five church leaders who managed to make their way to the city where under cover they studied and prayed together. At the close of the week Ray suggested they enter into a prayer covenant, setting aside each Friday as a time to pray for one another. Without hesitation, Goshu responded, "Of course you do mean fasting as well." That comment gave us clue that we had much to learn from them.

Early in the spring of 1991 the coalition forces from the north crossed the newly-completed bridge over the Blue Nile River and advanced on Addis Ababa. Their march took them right through the area of Wollega where our mission work had been concentrated. Heavy battles were waged in the previously quiet, isolated countryside. Colonel Mengistu Haile Mariam, in a last ditch effort to rally his troops, came to Kiremu, where he spent two nights at the former mission residence. When he saw that his army was defeated and the invading forces would eventually march on Addis Ababa, he returned to the city and subsequently fled to Zimbabwe. As a result of the overthrow of Marxism, the doors began to open for us to return to Ethiopia. That dream became a reality in July 1992 when we returned to pave the way for CMF to reenter and to return.

Insecurity continued in that western part of Ethiopia, so it was October before we received clearance to make the first trip back. We were able to see for ourselves what the years of oppression has wrought.

What we found was a church, not of four-thousand believers, nor of ten-thousand, but possibly twenty-thousand or more, having been under ground, meeting secretly in local village groups. The congregations had taken different forms, some aligning themselves with indigenous national churches with offices in Addis Ababa. Evidence of genuine faith and God's power at work among them were very obvious.

During the days of the Marxist regime the Christians were singled out for persecution and sometimes death. Churches were forbidden to meet in the vast majority of cases. The only weapons Christians had were spiritual. Fasting and prayer were essential to survival.

An elder in the church near Haro village shared his story. Ato Olana said that the Head of State, Colonel Mengistu Haile Mariam, had met with the First Secretary of the Communist Party for the Wollega Region. The Secretary had been very fierce in his opposition to the church and had been personally responsible for the closure of the churches and the imprisonment of leaders. The agreement between the President and the First Secretary was that fifty church leaders in the Horo-Gudiru District were to be singled out and killed under one guise or another.

Church leaders did not know of this threat but their prayers were accompanied with fasting as a regular practice. They prayed for God to give them boldness and that His name would be honored. After the communist government was toppled in May of 1991 the journal which included President Mengistu's signature authorizing the death of these fifty Christians was found and placed on exhibit. The man who related this story saw his own name on the list. God had used the coalition forces whose invasion route split the Horo-Gudiru District to make the fulfillment of the death order impossible. His means of deliverance are marvelous. The resource is prayer.

A Biblical Precedent

It should come as no surprise that the church survives by prayer and fasting, because that was the way the church began. This was how the missionary enterprise began. The beginning of Paul's life as a Christian was accompanied by prayer and fasting. Immediately after his experience on the Damascus road when he had a personal encounter with Christ, he was fasting and praying (Acts 9:9). That was when God sent Ananias to tell him what he needed to do.

In the thirteenth chapter of Acts we have the account of the commissioning of Barnabas and Saul for their missionary career. "In the church at Antioch there were prophets and teachers: Barnabas, Simeon called Niger, Lucius of Cyrene, Manaen (who had been brought up with Herod the tetrarch) and Saul" (Acts 13:1). The Antioch church was richly endowed with leaders--prophets and teachers. Prophets were gifted in bringing edification, exhortation, comfort and encouragement. Teachers taught effectively in a sustained ministry. While we do not know which of these five were prophets and which were teachers, we do know that they were all actively involved in the life of the church. Simeon was a common Hebrew name; Niger means "black." Perhaps he was Simeon of Cyrene, the one who carried the cross of Christ. Lucius was from Cyrene in North Africa. Manaen, whose name means "comforter", had grown up with the same Herod who had John the Baptist beheaded.

These men were scattered by the persecution of the believers, and through their witness, large numbers of Greeks in Antioch believed. The church in Jerusalem sent Barnabas, whose name means "Son of Encouragement", down to Antioch to investigate the reports of persecution. He went to Tarsus, found Saul, and together they taught great numbers of people (Acts 11:26).

"While they were worshiping and fasting..." From the text itself, it is not possible to tell whether "they" refers to the five prophets and teachers or to the entire Antioch church, but probably the whole church was involved, having come together for a specific purpose. Considering the cosmopolitan nature of the church at Antioch, that purpose could well have been the spreading of the gospel to other parts of the world.

"...worshiping the Lord and fasting..." The word used here for "worshiping" is the same one used for temple service. Though it cannot be narrowed to one specific kind of service, it is widely thought to be prayer since these two acts--prayer and fasting--are often associated (Macgregor 1954:167). As Harrow points out, "The church at Antioch laid aside even the demands of hunger to concentrate on serving God and receiving His guidance. It is a powerful example of how, when we wait in prayer, we can expect the Holy Spirit to reveal God's will" (1983:75).

"...the Holy Spirit said..." How did the Holy Spirit reveal His message? Was it through the prophets or through the "still small voice" to all of them? We do not know. But we do know that He made His message known so that all could understand what they were to do.

"Set apart for me Barnabas and Saul for the work to which I have called them." The work was not specifically stated, but understood by all to be that of carrying the gospel to those who had not heard.

"...so after they had fasted and prayed..." Stott's comments upon fasting and praying are helpful:

> As God's call was disclosed to them, their first reaction was to fast and pray, partly (it seems) to test God's call and partly to intercede for the two who were to be sent out. In neither reference to fasting does it occur alone. It is linked with worship in verse two and with prayer in verse three. Seldom, if ever, is fasting an end in itself. It is a negative action (abstention from food and other distractions) for the sake of a positive one (worshiping and praying). Then after they had fasted and prayed and so assured themselves of God's call and prepared themselves to obey it, they placed their hands on them and sent them off (1990:217).

Verse three of Acts 13 indicates that the church at Antioch sent Barnabas and Saul on this missionary journey. But verse four states that the two of them were sent on their way by the Holy Spirit. There are two different words used for "sent." In verse three the word means "released." Imagine how hard it was for the church at Antioch to give up two of her finest, most capable men who were no doubt needed where they were. The church let go its hold and released them from any claim on their lives. The word for "sent" in verse four means "to throw out" to "to thrust." The Holy Spirit impelled them to go. The church, in obedience and in waiting for God's leading, set them free.

> After further fasting and prayer, Barnabas and Saul were released and commissioned for their new service. Their colleagues laid their hands on them and sent them away with their blessing and good will. ... By this means the church of Antioch, through its leaders, expressed its fellowship with Barnabas and Saul and recognized them as its delegates or "apostles." They were sent out by the whole church, and it was to the whole church that they made their report when they returned to Antioch (Bruce 1988:246).

From the passage in the book of Acts we can see that the growth of Christianity was not due to human effort but came from God. Each new impetus to growth, each outreach, came from the direct command of the Holy Spirit.

The Ethiopia Church Depends Upon Prayer and Fasting

That the church does not expand by human means, but by the power of the Holy Spirit, is dramatically seen in the survival and expansion of the church in Ethiopia during the years of Marxist oppression. A sustaining practice which developed during those years was fasting and prayer. Houston is correct when he says,

> A valuable support in prayer is fasting. Fasting means to deprive ourselves of any activities or habits that are deeply ingrained into our lives, but popularly it means to go without food for a set length of time. As with prayer there is no particular value in fasting for it's own sake. It is practiced for greater ends than itself. It clears the mind, helps to concentrate on a specific subject, allowing us to subordinate our body's needs to our spiritual need for God. ... (It) is especially helpful in preparing for a special event, or in seeking guidance from God (1989:37).

During the years of Marxist oppression the church in Ethiopia learned the discipline of prayer and fasting. They pushed back from a full table and learned to fast and pray for a month at a time. This is borne out in the life of Afeta. When we first met him twenty-five years ago he was a new Christian. I can still remember the look of joy which radiated from his face as he described the transformation Christ had made in his life. Before he became a Christian he was such a bad person that people would run him away from their villages "like a hyena." They knew he was there for no good, but only to steal and cause trouble. As with the Apostle Paul, people were skeptical of this change and they were hesitant to trust him when he went back to these same villages to tell what had changed his life. He taught himself to read so that he could tell more than his own experience, reading and teaching directly from the Bible. His new faith was contagious.

When we saw Afeta again, after over eighteen years, his hair was white, his smile of joy in the Lord as infectious as ever. What had happened in this life in the intervening years?

Afeta endured those years with imprisonment and threats but emerged with his smile of joy. When asked for specific occasions that had called for intensive prayer and fasting, he referred to a time when he and several others leaders were imprisoned and fined. While Afeta and others from his village were in a prayer meeting, officials came and locked the door of the building--from the outside. They were caught red-handed. Fourteen of the men were brought to trial. Their crime: holding an unauthorized meeting. At the first trial they were fined $800, an impossible payment by people of so modest means.

There was a call to prayer and fasting. The case was transferred to a higher court. When the defendants appeared before the judge he asked if they were guilty or not guilty. The more timid ones responded, "Guilty." But when Afeta answered, he stated firmly, "Not guilty! I built the house. I led the meeting. I called the people together. But I am not guilty. I worshiped God before. I worship Him now. And I will worship him in the future." The men were all released without any payment other than their time in prison, due to the prayer and fasting of the church.

Another experience from the church should be cited. Three young men from the same family were away from home. Two were in the militia and one was away for schooling. Then the government was overthrown. During that time militia and regular soldiers died by the thousands. For a time it was dangerous for anyone to travel.

The three sons did not return, even after the surviving soldiers of the old regime began to come home. Were the three sons from the same family wiped out at the same time? But the church had been on its knees. The fast lasted for a month, and the three sons all returned unharmed.

Nouwen says, "We cannot plan, organize or manipulate God, but without careful disciplines we cannot receive him either" (1976:116). Tadela's testimony demonstrates this clearly. Tadela is a second-generation Christian. His father was one of the men who appeared at our door one day in the early 1970's asking for someone to come and teach him. He said, "We have a bible and there is someone from our village who can read, but we do not know very much." That was the beginning of a long and rewarding relationship.

When Ray went to their village he found a group of people who met every night to sing and pray and read the bible. Whatever they read they tried to put into practice. When they read, "Do not give dogs what is sacred", they stopped giving left-over bread to the dogs because the blessing had been said over it (Mt 7:6). When they read, "Watch out for those dogs..." they decided it was wrong to keep dogs at all (Phil 3:2). They had many questions about what they read and discussions went into the night. I remember vividly my first trip to that village. When we arrived after a long dusty walk, someone came with a clay jar of water and washed our feet. We were given the best facilities they had to offer, including the bed to sleep on which was located in the main house where the meeting was being held. The singing and praying lasted a long time; then the lesson and questions began. When I could not hold my eyes open any longer, I quietly crawled into my sleeping bag on the bed. The calf tied to the foot of the bed was making quiet noises. The questions and ensuing discussion continued. Some time later Ray crawled into his sleeping bag. The talking continued until the teacher no longer responded because he had fallen asleep. Then the people went quietly to their separate houses in the village.

What had happened in the intervening years in the church at Jebeca? My conversation with Tadela provided some answers. During the years of Marxist domination churches were closed and went underground, finding ways to meet undetected. In the village their tradition was to meet to drink coffee each morning. These meetings rotated from house to house and became times of prayer and worship.

Early in these years the practice of prayer and fasting began. Tadela said, "During the Marxist time, for seventeen years, we fully depended on fasting and prayer." The fasting and prayer consisted of two types--private and collective. Every month, as determined by the church leaders, there was a period of prayer and fasting for the church. Often this was observed before taking the Lord's Supper. The church leaders frequently fasted privately from Saturday morning until Sunday evening, devoting this time to prayer.

Tadela gave a specific instance. "A Christian man in the village took a wife, and a month later said he would not stay with her. No amount of counsel from the church elders would change his mind. The elders fasted and prayed secretly for eight days. Before the period of fasting was over, the man sent word that he wanted his wife back. Now they live together in love."

According to Tadela, the purpose of fasting is "to get strength from the Spirit." He said that during the seasons of fasting "many are healed, some are not, but there is always blessing."

When asked about personal fasting, Tadela said that his fasts usually lasted three to four days and were related to his specific requests to God. He added, "I do not feel hunger." Sometimes he and his wife pray and fast together for their home and their marriage. His summary comment was, "Spiritual joy and power come by fasting and prayer. We come to know God." His thoughts are echoed by Willard:

> Fasting confirms our utter dependence upon God by finding in Him a source of sustenance beyond food. Hence when Jesus directs us not to appear distressed and sad when we fast (Mt 6:16-18) he is not telling us to mislead those around us. He is instead explaining how we will feel. We really will not be sad. We are discovering that life is so much more than meat (1988:166-167).

In August of 1993 the first Bible course in over twenty years was held at Haro and was attended by fifty church leaders. This was followed by an area-wide conference where two-thousand gathered for worship. The day the Bible course began thirteen believers were arrested and imprisoned for refusing to take a tribal oath in which the names of non-gods were invoked. This was the first instance of persecution in this area since the fall of Marxism, and was imposed by the rising tide of ethnic tensions within the country.

The church leaders met and decided to take no overt action but rather to fast and pray. They were trained by the disciplines learned during the previous years of oppression. Within a week the thirteen men were released.

I like the way Andrew Murray explains the relationship between prayer and fasting. He says, "Prayer is the one hand with which we grasp the invisible; fasting, the other, with which we let loose and cast away the visible. ... Prayer is the reaching out after God and the unseen; fasting, the letting go of all that is seen and temporal. ... The soldier carries only what he needs for warfare, laying aside every weight" (1952:96).

The church in Ethiopia is a part of the continuing story begun in the book of Acts. We have much to learn from what they learned during their years of hardship and suffering. May we all commit ourselves to the expansion of God's kingdom.

> Stir me, Oh stir me, Lord
> Thy heart was stirred
> By loves intensest fire,
> 'Till Thou didst give
> Thine only Son,
> Thy best beloved One,
> E'en to the dreadful cross,
> That I might live.
> Stir me to give myself
> So back to Thee
> That Thou canst give Thyself again
> Through me (quoted in Roseveare 1980:145).

7

OPEN THE DOORS OF EFFECTIVE SERVICE

by Gail and Wayne Long

God ... had opened the door of faith to the Gentiles (Acts 14:27).

Introduction

You can be an effective urban evangelist by applying the principles found in the Acts of the Apostles. Today's world is a greatly expanded version of the world found in the first century A.D. The successful penetration of that world by the early Christians gives valuable lessons for us.

The book of Acts opens with Jesus challenging his disciples to be his witnesses everywhere. That mission begins in Jerusalem and radiates to the ends of the earth (Acts 1:8). The twenty-eight chapters of the book show the implementation of this grand design. The Gospel was carried to all major urban centers of the Roman Empire, then it spread to interior regions linked to the cities.

The spread of the Christian faith in the first century is phenomenal. How those men and women accomplished such a feat is the story of the Acts of the Apostles. The acts of Peter, Paul and others begin in Jerusalem and end in Rome. Their recorded activities take place in fifty-seven different cities and towns.

Let us look at what took place and see the principles of effective evangelism. These principles enabled dedicated people to carry the Good News to the ends of the earth in their generation.

The Gospel Goes to Antioch

Persecution of believers in Jerusalem forced them to flee that city and go to distant places (Acts 11:19-20). Men and women hastily left Jerusalem for safer havens. Some returned to former homes left years before. Others went to live with relatives and acquaintances. Some went to Phoenicia and Cyprus, others went to Antioch.

Antioch in the first century was a magnificent city. It was the third largest city of the Roman Empire. It traced its proud history from Alexander the Great. His general, Seleucius, made Antioch his capital, a wise choice. Situated between the Lebanese and Tarsus mountains, it was a transportation hub. Caravan routes fanned out in every direction. The Orontes River emptied into the Mediterranean only fifteen miles away. Trade flourished. Being the seat of government only increased its population. It also became a religious center with its beautiful temple to the goddess Daphne. People from every corner of the world could be found in its markets, residential sectors and public places. This center was a safe haven for the evacuees fleeing from persecution in Jerusalem.

The followers of Jesus began holding regular meetings. They studied the Apostle's teachings and the Old Testament. They prayed together and celebrated the Lord's Supper. They enjoyed great fellowship.

Who were these people? No one knows, but perhaps they were led by Nicholas or were related to him (Acts 6:5). Through their efforts the new congregation grew rapidly. At first they spoke only to Jews, but soon non-Jews also heard the message and accepted it wholeheartedly (Acts 11:19-20). The Gospel was not intended for, nor could not be contained within just one ethnic group. Antioch proved to be fertile ground for church growth.

At this point in the story one of two things happened. One, the new group desired greater leadership and sent word back to Jerusalem for help. Or two, the Jerusalem group, upon hearing about the congregation in Antioch, determined to send some of their own leadership to strengthen the new church.

The man chosen by the Jerusalem church to go to the new work in Antioch was Barnabas. Evidence of his calling and love for the Lord's work dates back to the earliest days of the church in Jerusalem. He was a generous person; selling the field he owned and bringing the money to put at the feet of the apostles (Acts 4:36-37). He was a good man, full of the Holy Spirit and faith, and he encouraged the new congregation in Antioch. Under encouragement from Barnabas, a great many people were brought to the Lord (Acts 11:24).

The success of the new church led Barnabas to see that he needed help. He sought out the man he had met several years earlier and who now resided in Tarsus, some seventy-five miles away. Barnabas arranged passage to Tarsus and placed the need of the new ministry before Paul. He challenged the tentmaker to a new work in the capital, and Paul accepted.

Barnabas and Paul ministered together for a year. They preached and taught incessantly. The Lord blessed their efforts and many lives were touched. The believers were first called Christians at Antioch. The historian Latourette writes, "It was at Antioch, fittingly, that the followers of Jesus were first given the distinctive designation by which they have ever since been known, Christian. The word, itself Greek, symbolized the emergence of the new faith into the wider world" (1953:68). Whereas before the believers of Jesus had been called "followers of the way", or other names, now they were called "Christians". Even King Agrippa confirmed the new designation when Paul tried to convert him (Acts 26:28).

During this first ministry of Paul and Barnabas, a prophet named Agabus came to Antioch from Jerusalem predicting a great famine. The congregation responded with an offering and asked Paul and Barnabas to carry the money to Jerusalem and give it to the leaders of the church to distribute to those in need. By their benevolent works, they showed their concern for others.

The Antioch church showed this same concern for others by setting aside Paul and Barnabas as their missionaries and sending them out to speak the words of truth to the Gentiles. The Holy Spirit had called them to a ministry to the Gentiles and the Antioch church confirmed this call. The church lost little time in sending out these men of faith on a journey that would take them to Cyprus, Lycia, Pamphylia and Lycaonia.

Their journey took months to complete, and then they returned to report to the church in Antioch. They shared the news of everything that had taken place. The two co-workers then began another ministry with the fast growing church. But this time a controversy arose to plague their efforts.

The problem was one which often takes place when the Gospel takes root in a different culture. The issue concerned the heart of the Christian faith--how is the essence of Christianity to be distinguished from that which is cultural practice? Jewish Christians came from Jerusalem insisting that the believers in Antioch must become Jews first before they become Christians. For those from Antioch, this would mean upholding the Jewish cultural practices of circumcision, dietary and food laws, following of Jewish holidays and observance of the law as it was currently being interpreted.

As the controversy raged, Peter visited the Antioch church. His love for Jesus was unquestioned. It was through him that the door of the church was first opened to the Gentiles (Acts 10). When he first arrived he mingled gladly with the church. But when the critical Jewish Christians arrived from Jerusalem, Peter withdrew his fellowship from the Gentile Christians. It was then that Paul felt compelled to confront Peter (Gal 2:11-14).

After much discussion, the decision was made to send a delegation to Jerusalem to discuss the issue. Paul was among those chosen. The leaders from Jerusalem reached the following conclusion: 1) it should not be difficult for the Gentiles who are turning to God (Acts 15:19); and 2) a letter should be written to those in Antioch telling them to refrain from certain practices (Acts 15:20). Paul, along with Barnabas, Judas and Silas, returned to Antioch to deliver the letter and advice of the Jerusalem council.

Once back in Antioch Paul and Barnabas continued to minister in the city. Hearing once again the call to mission service, the two missionaries determined to revisit the places and congregations launched during their first tour. The second missionary journey lasted many months, but once again Paul returned to the church at Antioch.

Then again, Paul sets out from Antioch for a third missionary journey. His ministry now takes a different turn, and he never returns to Antioch. The ministry in Antioch continued to grow. The city's position as the gateway to the Tigris-Euphrates river valley and the ancient city of Damascus allowed the gospel to flow freely into the interior. Though use of the Greek language continued, the Gospel also made inroads into the dominant Syrian speaking areas. The Gospels were translated and much Christian literature was produced in that language.

Lessons To Be Learned

The growth of the church in Antioch provides timeless lessons for those who wish to be involved in urban evangelism today. We will enumerate seven such lessons.

1. Commit Your Life to the Lordship of Jesus Christ

While the call to commit yourself to the Lordship of Jesus Christ may sound trite, it is not. Consecration to Jesus Christ is the key to effective urban work--wherever it takes place. When Jesus said, "I will build my church," He spoke to his innermost circle of disciples. It would be through them that salvation would be preached to lost people. They were to be the divinely appointed means by which the Good News would conquer the hearts of urban multitudes.

The seed of the Gospel was planted in Syrian soil because nameless people were so committed to Jesus that they began Christian cells in the Roman Empire's third largest city. The leader of that work was Barnabas, a man whose dedication led him to sell his goods and lay them at the feet of the apostles. Later he was asked to oversee the distribution of funds for needy widows and orphans.

As the work grew Barnabas chose Paul, another whose commitment to Christ was beyond question. Paul left Damascus in a basket at night. When his sojourn in Jerusalem was curtailed by threats and plotting, Paul transferred his efforts to Tarsus. When Barnabas recruited him, he left Tarsus to labor in Antioch.

The Lord's claim on my husband's life came through the ministry of Harry E. Berg. Harry taught him the simple steps of personal commitment to Christ. Compellingly he taught about the desire of the crowd on the Day of Pentecost. My husband learned about Saul, Cornelius, the Ethiopian treasurer, Lydia and the jailer at Philippi. He too confessed his faith like Peter, saying, "I believe that Jesus is the Christ, the Son of the living God." In a small people movement, his brother, three cousins, his grandmother and he were baptized into Christ. It was a decisive moment in his life. He has never regretted the decision to follow Jesus Christ wherever he leads. In our cross cultural work in Brazil and in the northeastern United States, that one thing stands paramount. Church planting rises and falls around persons who are strongly committed to Christ.

The work is difficult. Locating people in today's city is a challenge. Hectic schedules, shift work, transportation, ethnic mix--all make it difficult to locate the urban person and present the eternal claims of Christ. Moral failure, backsliding, and anonymity all work against the urban minister. Therefore, an intense commitment to Christ is one of the keys to successful urban work.

2. Go Where the Lord is Leading You

The urban worker must be willing to go as the Great Commission dictates. No one becomes a Christian unless someone is willing to go, find, meet, become acquainted and persuade that person to follow Christ. Who is to go?

Ordinary Christians

Luke tells us, "On that day a great persecution broke out against the church at Jerusalem, and all except the apostles were scattered throughout Judea and Samaria" (Acts 8:1). These unnamed ordinary Christians took the faith to Alexandria, Rome and Antioch. They preached wherever they went.

The Evangelical Christian Church in Worcester, Massachusetts is an illustration of the power of ordinary people to produce church growth. Josimar Gouvea, pastor of the church, left the congregation to update his immigration documents. The consul in Brazil denied his request for a visa, so the congregation was left without a pastor. Pastor Josimar sent a letter outlining the duties of various persons in the church and they went to work.

Almost immediately the church began to grow. In the six months the pastor has been absent, the attendance of this new congregation doubled. The church is now wrestling with the problem of the absence of pastoral leadership. Some people say, "We need a pastor to lead us," and "A pastor will help us grow." But one of the laymen leading the church during the interim says, "No pastor can make the church grow. It is our job to make the church grow." This young believer puts into words a key element in urban church growth--it must be the priority of local Christians to make disciples of all persons.

Sabastiana Nogueira of Brazil is a diminutive and dynamic person. She became a Christian while still an unwed mother. A beautiful grace and love for Christ and others characterizes her life.

Following her conversion, she became an active worker for Christ. She taught Sunday School, worked with young people, prepared special programs and visited other people extensively.

It was a happy day when she and the father of her child were wed. He asked her to join him in Sao Paulo where he lived. She went. Her sister lived in a *favela,* a poor temporary housing area. Sabastiana's heart reached out to the people who lived in Vila Sao Jose as the *favela* was called. She resolved to do something.

Sabastiana began holding regular meetings for Bible study, praise and worship. She contacted her church in Campinas, some 80 kilometers away, for help. A caravan was organized, and a public meeting was held in front of her sister's small home. An offering was collected, which began a fund to build a small chapel. The women and children worked in the construction. The small chapel has continued to grow and prosper. Its life is due to the effort of a small woman who resolved to labor in the cause of Christ.

Regional Evangelists

In the early church there were several evangelists who had a regional ministry. Philip's ministry in Acts 8 is typical. Led by the Spirit, Philip ministers in the region of Samaria. His work in the capital city is especially blessed as many persons became Christians. Churches are founded and the Gospel is effectively preached; an excellent example of a church ministering in its region. From the mother church in Jerusalem the Gospel radiated out to the nearby areas.

Several years ago our family was vacationing on the Brazilian coast near the tourist town of Caraguatatuba. Next to the campground was a church. We noticed that it was a Holiness Church. The Holiness Church in Brazil was started by Japanese immigrants. Around the camp there were extensive farms owned by Japanese immigrants. When Sunday arrived we went to church knowing that the service would probably be in Japanese.

When we arrived, the church was packed. There were people flowing out of the church onto the steps and beyond. As we were obviously visitors, the people made a place for us up at the front. The preacher and the leaders were Japanese, but the congregation was predominantly Brazilian farmers from the surrounding farms.

During the week my husband wanted to get better acquainted with the preacher, so he went to visit. Wayne asked the preacher when he was going to build a larger building to accommodate all of the people coming to the meetings. He smiled at Wayne and said, "I am not going to enlarge this building. My plan is to build a building like this in every district throughout this region." As we visited I learned that this congregation already had twenty-three preaching points. Every week the preacher sent out mission teams to evangelize and conduct services in places as far away as the outskirts of metropolitan Sao Paulo. The Holiness preacher in Caraguatatuba was effectively evangelizing his entire region for the Kingdom of God.

Latter Day Apostles, or "Sent Ones"

Since one of the meanings of the word "apostle" is "sent one," I believe cross cultural workers are latter day apostles. Missions have always been an interest to us. As a youth, Wayne was inspired by visiting missionaries. John and Mabel Ross captivated him with their messages about Zaire. In his undergraduate days he was privileged to meet Dr. Donald McGavran and to room with Dr. Alan Tippett, both involved with the Church Growth Movement. These associations fueled Wayne's interest in missions.

Serving in our first full time pastorate in Dallas, Texas, Wayne felt a need to do more in the area of missions. He contacted a mission organization on behalf of our church and was urged to personally consider a ministry in Brazil. He had never really thought about the possibility of mission service for himself. It was a new idea. He meditated upon the possibility and prayed, the result being an affirmation of his decision to follow Christ wherever He led. "If He wanted me to serve, I would go. But would my wife Gail agree?"

Wayne approached me with the challenge of going to Brazil. "Would you like to do this?" he asked. I replied, "That is fine with me. Let's go." Our decisiveness put us into action. After further schooling, we arrived in Brazil in early 1976. The next seven years were spent in evangelism and church planting among the Brazilian peoples. Our questions about the acceptance of an American preaching Christ to Brazilian people were answered. People were won to Christ and churches were planted.

A majority of the unwon people in this world will never be won unless people leave their familiar and comfortable surroundings and go with the Good News of Christ to those who live around them. Others will have wider regional ministries. Still others must go into new and uncharted areas to establish Gospel beachheads.

3. Take Full Advantage of Living Relationships

Urban workers must maximize living relationships. The Gospel naturally travels along the living relationships of people. Birds of a feather do flock together, and people like to become Christians without having to cross barriers. When the tax collector Matthew decided to follow Jesus, the first thing he did was to invite his friends and associates to meet the Master (Lk 5:29). Andrew, the brother of Simon Peter, was one who had left his work to follow Jesus. The first thing that Andrew did was to find his brother Simon and tell him, " 'We have found the Messiah.' And he brought him to Jesus" (Jn 1:41-42).

The Gospel traveled along similar channels when it came to Antioch. In the great scattering which occurred as a result of the Jerusalem persecution, it was only natural that the Christians fled to live with their relatives in Tyre, Cyprus and Antioch.

In today's urban centers the missionary is wise who follows the living links of family and friendship. The question is, "How do I make my initial contacts?" Fortunately for us in the United States, the US Census has done a lot of the work. One of the questions which was asked in the 1990 Census was, "What language is spoken at home?" Whether you are looking for Laotian or Portuguese, the answer is as near as your local census depository. Your research will lead you from state summaries to county summaries. Every county is broken up into census tracts. In large urban areas the tracks are even broken into city block groupings. Maps of the block groups and census tracts are available. You can know with a high degree of certainty the exact location of the people you seek.

These people are also known by many other services and organizations. They buy particular foods and trade in specialty stores. They get driver's licenses and go to hospitals. They send money back to their family and friends in the old home area. They are able to travel and visit their friends. All of these avenues provide fruitful ways to locate the people to whom God is calling you to minister.

Once you have located the people, the most difficult part of your effort begins--preaching the Good News to them. It is hard when you are on the outside and have not yet gained an entrance into the group. The first few years were an uphill battle for the Hisportic Christian Mission. In Pawtucket, where we began, our successes during the first several years were minimal. Now, we have a core group of persons within the ethnic group.

In 1993 each of the congregations we have been involved with conducted a "Bring-A-Friend" Sunday service. Each Christian was to bring a non-Christian friend to a typical worship service. No Christians were to be invited. The results were amazing. Attendance doubled. But better than that, the persons in attendance were not Christians. Through taking advantage of the principle of living relationships we were able to reach out to non-believers in a decisive way.

4. Recognize and Work Within the Ethnic Realities

Reading through the book of Acts provides a catalog of diverse ethnic groups. The crowd at Jerusalem described in the second chapter, lists persons from almost every area of the Greco- Roman world. The issue with the widows and orphans in chapter six reveals a distinction between Hebrew and Greek-speaking Jews. In chapter eight Samaritans and Ethiopians are mentioned.

In Antioch we read of Jews and God-fearing Greeks. Among the latter the message of Christ finds fertile ground. The Gentile Greeks receive the message in a marvelous way. Soon they are the dominant group in the church.

The first cross cultural effort in our own ministry was the Iglesia Cristiana del Pueblo, a Spanish language ministry focused on the Cubans living in the Lakewood District of Dallas, Texas. The group also included Mexicans, Dominicans and a few other Spanish speaking groups. The dominant group was the Cubans. They ran the show. The services bore an unmistakable Cuban flavor. Worship must always be in the heart language of the people--the language that the people fight in and make love in!

Worship and fellowship activities must also fit into the cultural milieu. Our mission's congregations have their principal worship services on Sunday evenings. In Brazil the primary service is also Sunday evening because Sunday morning is for Sunday school. This pattern fits with the immigrant lifestyle because many work until 5 p.m. on Sundays. When snacks are served, they are the familiar ethnic foods that the people know and enjoy.

In today's cosmopolitan urban areas it is difficult for a church to reach out to the diverse peoples around it. The best example we have found is the First Baptist Church of Flushing, New York. This church is effectively serving an ethnically diverse community. Ethnic and language-based worship services have been organized. The separate services are conducted in Spanish, Portuguese, Mandarin, Cantonese, West Indian, Jewish and one for the hearing impaired. All of the related groups are considered part of First Baptist Church, and each one has special workers assigned to it. Christian workers who seek to minister in today's urban world must work within the ethnic realities present.

5. Equip Others for Christian Ministry

Ultimately, the worker's efforts will rise or fall on the success of his or her efforts to recruit, train and deploy leadership. Nowhere is this more critical than in the urban setting.

The founders of the Jerusalem church recognized the need for training and growth, not only in their own congregation but also in their daughter church in Antioch. Barnabas was chosen and sent to Antioch to train those who were a part of the growing fellowship. Soon it became apparent that more help was needed. Barnabas went and recruited Paul to join him in the ministry.

Paul displayed a marvelous gift for recruiting and mobilizing laypersons, as can be seen from the people he mentions: Sopater from Berea; Aristarcus and Secundus from Thessalonica; Gaius and Timothy from Derbe; and Tychicus and Trophimus from the province of Asia.

Julio Neris, a fine young Brazilian pastor, started the Mount Sinai Bible Institute. He has trained six people now for advanced leadership roles. Earl Haubner, a missionary from central Brazil, made it his practice to provide advanced training on Sunday mornings at 7:30 a.m. Maintaining this program over the years has produced a large pool of capable leaders for the Brazilian churches. The person who would effectively minister in today's urban setting will develop a means of training and equipping others for ministry.

6. Seek Creative Ways to Overcome Property Barriers

The securing of property is often a barrier to Christian growth. New churches in urban areas struggle to find adequate meeting places. Many are forced to disband because they cannot find acceptable places to worship and teach. The early church successfully overcame the property barrier, and today's churches must do the same.

There are fifty-four references to Jerusalem in the book of Acts. It is undeniably the center of early Christianity. When the city was destroyed in 70 A.D. by the Romans, Christianity did not come to an end. A careful reading of the book of Acts shows that the property barrier was overcome. The apostles taught in synagogues, in homes, in the Temple, in a lecture hall, in an open forum, and along the river banks.

In our own ministry we have served groups and conducted meetings in many different places. In Brazil we have conducted meetings in government youth training facilities, housing projects, community halls, school buildings, brick drying sheds and on street corners.

Today our mission in America has baptized 200 Portuguese speaking persons. Its cooperating congregations serve about 1200 people. None of these churches have their own building. All rent existing facilities.

Urban ministry will be stifled if we need to purchase buildings for all of the congregations that need to be formed. Effective church workers will find creative ways to overcome the property barrier. However, this is an expensive part of urban ministry. Building rents are very high.

7. Intentionally Cross the Linguistic and Cultural Obstacles

We have already noted the importance of working within the ethnic realities present in the urban situation. Like-minded people need to be sought out and evangelized aggressively. Every effort needs to be made to enable them to win their community for Christ. The gospel is for all people. While we focus on one people we cannot forget that Christ died for all. A single ethnic church must be taught to reach beyond their own group. The linguistic and cultural barriers which separate people must be crossed with the Gospel message.

The intentional crossing of linguistic and cultural barriers gave rise to the church in Antioch. Greek-speaking Jews spoke to their Gentile friends. The new church in the Syrian capital possessed the mind of Christ. They sent Paul and Barnabas off to Europe. These missionaries followed the roads that led into the Mesopotamian Valley. Churches were soon formed in Damascus, Babylon, Palmyra, Media and Elam. The Bible was translated into Syrian--the principal language of the area.

Today, more than any other time in history, urban churches must reach beyond their own group to those who live nearby but who are culturally different. In Providence, Rhode Island, fifty-five different languages are spoken in the public schools. A mono-linguistic and mono-cultural church will not adequately minister to the increasing diversity of the population.

Business and commerce has recognized this need. Their leaders say that the days of mass communication are over. The successful businesses of the future will focus on niche marketing. They will recognize and target multiple groupings of people. Those who follow such a program will be the business successes while others lag behind.

Such a fundamental change in our society has not escaped the church. Several years ago in Houston the National Convocation on Evangelizing Ethnic America was convened. The message was simple. The future is ethnic. American Christians need to mobilize to meet this need if we are ever to be witnesses in Jerusalem, Judea, Samaria and to the ends of the earth.

What is happening in urban American is also happening in Europe, and in Asia and in Africa. The urban concentrations of people are increasingly diverse.

The missionary message of the book of Acts comes alive in today's world. The Gospel was carried to all major urban centers of the Roman Empire. As we follow these timeless principles we will see effective doors of Christian ministry open. The urgency of the hour is to cross the linguistic and cultural obstacles which divide people and claim them for Christ.

8

NO DISTINCTION BETWEEN US AND THEM

by Donald S. Tingle

Some men came down from Judea to Antioch and were teaching the brothers: "Unless you are circumcised, according to the custom taught by Moses, you cannot be saved." This brought Paul and Barnabas into sharp dispute and debate with them. So Paul and Barnabas were appointed, along with some other believers, to go up to Jerusalem to see the apostles and elders about this question. The church sent them on their way, and as they traveled through Phoenicia and Samaria, they told how the Gentiles had been converted. This news made all the brothers very glad. When they came to Jerusalem, they were welcomed by the church and the apostles and elders, to whom they reported everything God had done through them.

Then some of the believers who belonged to the party of the Pharisees stood up and said, "The Gentiles must be circumcised and required to obey the law of Moses."

The apostles and elders met to consider this question. After much discussion, Peter got up and addressed them: "Brothers, you know that some time ago God made a choice among you that the Gentiles might hear from my lips the message of the gospel and believe. God, who knows the heart, showed that he accepted them by giving the Holy Spirit to them, just as he did to us. He made no distinction between us and them, for he purified their hearts by faith. Now then, why do you try to test God by putting on the necks of the disciples a yoke that neither we nor our fathers have been able to bear? No! We believe it is through the grace of our Lord Jesus that we are saved, just as they are" (Acts 15:1-11).

99

God's truth is not limited to any one culture. The Gospel is for all humanity, but it is always received within a specific cultural context. This context includes a people's language, customs, heritage, worldview, religion and all the other things we find in a culture.

The Practice of Contextualization

Contextualization may seem like a technical term in missions studies which would be difficult to understand. However, its basic concept is rather simple. It addresses the context in which people live. In other words it pays serious attention to the culture of the people when the Gospel is presented to them, so that they will understand rather than misunderstand the message. It also represents the way we endeavor to introduce new ideas to another culture. Whether we stop to think about it or not, whenever we communicate cross-culturally we are contextualizing. Whenever our culture adopts an idea which was once foreign to it, we are contextualizing. Everybody contextualizes. In missions studies the question is--How can we contextualize the Gospel message most effectively to help churches grow in other cultures?

God effectively established the church by contextualization in the beginning. Jesus did not expect Jews who became his disciples to abandon all their customs. On the contrary he said, "Therefore every teacher of the law who has been instructed about the kingdom of heaven is like the owner of a house who brings out of his storeroom new treasures as well as old" (Mt 13:52). When the church was first established among Jewish believers, they met for worship in the temple, synagogues and homes. Their Jewish customs and Hebrew patterns of thinking were not abandoned, but rather they were reinterpreted in the light of Christ. When predominantly Gentile churches came into existence, they did not follow all the customs of their Jewish brothers and sisters, but Christ became Lord of their Gentile ways of thinking and living. The worldviews of both Jews and Gentiles were changed when Christ became the Lord of their worlds. Although Paul was speaking about sin and speculations which keep people from God, his aim to "take captive every thought to make it obedient to Christ" applied equally well to the process of Christ becoming Lord within each cultural perspective (2 Co 10:5).

The Early Church Crossing Cultural Barriers

Contextualizing the Gospel was often a painful process for the early church, as is seen in the case of Antioch of Syria. It was the third largest city of the Roman Empire and was home to a sizable Jewish community. When the church in Jerusalem was scattered as a result of persecution (Acts 8:1-4), some came to Antioch "telling the message only to Jews", which was customary at that time (Acts 11:19). However, that was to change through the efforts of some Jewish disciples who were from Cyprus and Cyrene. They began to speak "to Greeks also, telling them the good news about the Lord Jesus" (Acts 11:20).

Although the Gentile Cornelius and his household had already become disciples of Christ in Caesarea (Acts 10), we have no record of a concerted effort by a church to reach Gentiles with the Gospel before this attempt by some Jews in Antioch. Their efforts met with success. Luke reported, "The Lord's hand was with them, and a great number of people believed and turned to the Lord" (Acts 11:21).

The Antioch church expanded its efforts to reach Gentiles with the Gospel when it was directed by the Holy Spirit to send Paul and Barnabas on their first missionary journey (Acts 13:1-3). After Paul and Barnabas were sent out, they first preached the message to the Jewish residents in various cities until they came to Pisidian Antioch (not to be confused with the Antioch of Syria from which they were sent). There they met stiff opposition from Jews. They told these opponents, "We had to speak the word of God to you first. Since you reject it and do not consider yourselves worthy of eternal life, we now turn to the Gentiles" (Acts 13:46).

The Gentiles welcomed the news and a number of them throughout the whole region responded to the Gospel. As Paul and Barnabas continued their journey to other cities, a great multitude of both Jews and Gentiles became believers. Their preaching to the Jews emphasized different themes when compared to their preaching to the Gentiles although they were calling both groups to accept the same Gospel (see Acts 13:13-41 and Acts 14:8-18). When Paul and Barnabas returned to Antioch of Syria they reported to the church "all that God had done through them and how he had opened the door of faith to the Gentiles" (Acts 14:27).

Jewish Traditions for Gentile Converts?

The missionary minded church in Antioch of Syria consisted of both Jewish and Gentile believers, and each group had its own customs. This led to tensions within the church which are recorded in Acts 15:1-29. Judea, and especially the mother church in Jerusalem, rose up as the bastion of Jewish Christianity in the face of Gentile innovations. Some within the Judean church came to Antioch to make sure that Gentile traditions did not endanger faithful adherence to Jewish traditions. They taught, "Unless you are circumcised, according to the custom taught by Moses, you cannot be saved" (Acts 15:1). The greatest danger in this ultimatum was the claim that salvation was dependent on obeying the law of Moses rather than through the grace of God in Jesus Christ.

A secondary concern was that this negated the universal nature of God's grace. Paul later addressed this concern when he linked justification by faith for Gentiles with Abraham's righteousness by faith; Abraham, who was not a Jew, was to be the one through whom all nations would be blessed. Paul affirmed that the Jews did not have a monopoly on Abraham; not only was he the physical father of more than one nation, but on a spiritual level, "those who believe are children of Abraham" (Gal 3:7). Paul and Barnabas believed that these Jewish disciples who had come to Antioch had distorted God's intention for the Gospel, and they intensely debated the issue with them.

Paul and Barnabas Go to Jerusalem for Advice

The church decided to send Paul and Barnabas and certain other leaders in the church to Jerusalem to get guidance from the apostles and elders on this issue. As Paul and Barnabas traveled through Phoenicia and Samaria toward Jerusalem, they visited believers and described in detail the conversion of the Gentiles. These disciples rejoiced to know that the work of God among the Gentiles which began in their geographical neighborhood with the conversion of Cornelius and his household had now spread to more distant regions as well.

The apostles and elders in Jerusalem met to hear the dispute. After much debate, Peter stood up and reminded them that God had sent him to preach to the Gentiles when he went to Cornelius' home, that God gave them the Holy Spirit just as he had done to Jewish believers, and that "He made no distinction between us and them, for he purified their hearts by faith" (Acts 15:9). He said they should not test God by demanding that Gentiles carry the burden of the Law of Moses when neither the Jewish disciples of Christ nor their fathers were able to carry it adequately. The issue was salvation. Must Gentiles be circumcised and observe the Law of Moses to be saved? Peter responded with an emphatic "No!" He said, "We believe it is through the grace of our Lord Jesus that we are saved, just as they are" (Acts 15:11).

The Advice of the Jerusalem Council

James agreed with Peter. He saw the Gentile inclusion in the church as a fulfillment of the Prophet who wrote, "I will return and rebuild David's fallen tent... that the remnant of men may seek the Lord, and all the Gentiles who bear my name" (Acts 15:16-17). So this inclusion of Gentiles fulfilled the end times expectation of the Old Testament rather than making a break with God's plan. James then gave some simple guidelines for the Gentiles to follow, and the apostles and elders with the support of the church relayed these guidelines to the Antioch Christians. They were to "abstain from food sacrificed to idols, from blood, from the meat of strangled animals and from sexual immorality" (Acts 15:29).

This may seem like a strange list of things to avoid. It is easy to see why they were directed to avoid idolatry and sexual impurity, but why avoid eating blood or animals which had not been properly bled when slaughtered? It was more than just a way of saying to the Gentiles, "Don't eat food which disgusts Jewish believers," because the Gentile Christians were never commanded to avoid all forms of non-kosher food. Adherence to the dietary part of this list may not have been necessary for salvation, but it was crucial for fellowship between Jews and Gentiles. It appears to be a reminder to both sides that God once established a covenant with all of humanity through Noah, and now all of humanity is once again reunited with God through the new covenant in Christ (Gen 9:4-6).

Paul's Guiding Principle

The tendency to make everybody in the church follow Jewish customs was terribly difficult to resist. Peter came to Antioch and shared meals with the Gentiles, but when some people close to James arrived in the city Peter withdrew from the Gentiles out of fear of the "party of the circumcision." The rest of the Jewish believers in the church followed Peter's example, including Paul's missionary companion Barnabas. Paul had to rebuke Peter in the presence of the whole group, so that the whole group would return to the unity of faith based on grace (Gal 2:11-21).

Even after that rift was mended, however, some ultra-zealous Jewish believers continued to try to compel Gentiles to be circumcised according to the Mosaic law. Weaker Christians went along with them "to avoid being persecuted for the cross of Christ" (Gal 6:12). Paul did not give in to the pressures, and he was attacked for his position. He said, "I bear on my body the marks of Jesus" (Gal 6:17).

At first glance it seems odd that after Paul endured such hardships for his defense of the message of salvation by grace apart from the Law of Moses, he would on occasion be so ready to obey Jewish customs. Some have felt that he was indecisive or that he succumbed to the pressures of certain Jewish leaders. But I believe that he was faithfully following a guiding principle in his Christian witness:

> Though I am free and belong to no man, I make myself a slave to everyone to win as many as possible. To the Jews I became like a Jew, to win the Jews. To those under the law I became like one under the law (though I myself am not under the law), so as to win those under the law. To those not having the law I became like one not having the law (though I am not free from God's law but am under Christ's law), so as to win those not having the law. To the weak I became weak. I have become all things to all men so that by all possible means I might save some. I do all this for the sake of the gospel, that I may share in its blessings (1 Co 9:19-23).

Paul also told others to follow this pattern where possible. He wrote, "Do not cause anyone to stumble, whether Jews, Greeks or the Church of God--even as I try to please everybody in every way. For I am not seeking my own good but the good of many, so that they may be saved" (1 Co 10:32-33).

Paul Set Limitations

Obviously Paul could not please people of other faiths when the Gospel came into direct conflict with sin or falsehood. Demetrius, a silversmith who made shrines of the Ephesian goddess Artemis, started a riot when Paul's preaching caused sales of idols to drop (Acts 19:23-41). Jews in the temple in Jerusalem cried for Paul's execution when he testified that the Lord Jesus appeared to him in a trance and told him, "Go; I will send you far away to the Gentiles" (Acts 22:21). Claiming to receive a call from God to cross-cultural ministry was a crime worthy of death in the minds of this crowd.

Although Paul was not always able to please Gentiles and Jews in all matters, he accommodated himself to both groups where he saw no conflict with the message of the Gospel. This was neither indecision nor hypocrisy on his part. It was rather an intense commitment to let the message of the Gospel shine through in whatever context, be it Jewish or Gentile, so clearly that people would be able to understand it when they responded. Whether their response was submission to God in faith or rebellion against the message of God, Paul wanted to make sure that neither he nor the manner in which he presented the message to the hearer was a stumbling-block; if a person stumbles, it must only be at Jesus Christ and his Gospel, not the messenger or the method.

Paul, inasmuch as was possible, became "like a Jew to win the Jews" (1 Co 9:20). He lived as one under the Law of Moses even though he knew that the Law of Moses could not give life; he knew the Law pointed out our sinfulness so that we might turn to Christ for justification before God (Gal 3:19-24). Although he did not rely on obedience to the Law for salvation, he did not object to submitting to the practices of the Law as an act of worship and as a means of helping win Jews to faith in Christ.

The New Testament records several examples of this in Paul's life. While Paul fought against linking circumcision with salvation, he had no objection in continuing this tradition among Jewish Christians (Acts 16:1-3). Following opposition from Jewish leaders, he made a vow which concluded with the shaving of his head, likely the Jewish Nazirite vow (Acts 18:18). Later he engaged in Jewish purification rites and paid for the Temple sacrifices offered by four other men (Acts 21:20-26).

Paul knew that salvation could not be obtained by these customs, but he still participated in these rituals. He did it so that he might better identify with Jewish Christians, and perhaps it would help him establish a level of credibility for witnessing to Jews who had not yet accepted Christ.

But I believe Paul had more integrity than merely to go through meaningless rituals to gain a psychological advantage over a Jewish audience. He must also have made this event an act of worship and praise to God's glory; otherwise, he would have been acting hypocritically. It was not wrong for Paul to participate in these Jewish practices as long as he did not confuse them with salvation according to the Gospel. These events supplemented his spiritual life in Christ instead of supplanting his life in Christ.

The Respect of Other's Beliefs

Paul, as much as possible, became like the Gentiles. He ate with the Gentiles and fought for freedom from the customs of Moses for the Gentiles. He also was familiar with Gentile literature and maxims. He quoted from a Gentile poet (Acts 17:28) and from a Gentile prophet (Tit 1:12) to communicate spiritual truth. He did not explain the origin of these truths; nor did he qualify his quotation from a Gentile prophet by saying that the prophet was true in some areas and false in others. He simply quoted extra-biblical sources when it supported God's message.[1]

Paul even avoided blaspheming (speaking evil against) the goddess Artemis of the Ephesians (Acts 19:37). Instead of attacking the religious beliefs and practices of the Ephesians, he concentrated on proclaiming Christ. Paul could have verbally abused the image of Artemis as a multi-breasted monstrosity, her priests as greedy charlatans, and her worshipers as fools, but instead he concentrated on showing a better way in gentleness. Large numbers of people in Ephesus turned from idolatry as they were drawn to the light of the Gospel. No abusive speech against Artemis was needed; love and respect for people when the truth was presented proved to be sufficient.

Contextualization is Biblical

This survey of Biblical material related to contextualization shows that the process is not foreign to the church but was there from the beginning. The Gospel always takes root in a specific context, a particular cultural framework, whether it is first century Jerusalem or the United States today. But it is still the same Gospel working in all of us throughout church history to bring us to maturity in Christ.

Contextualization exists to make the Gospel plain to those who think and feel differently from people in our culture. I like what John V. Taylor wrote about the need for us to see the world through the eyes of people of other faiths in their cultures:

> I must be patient enough to listen and learn until I begin to see the world through his eyes. At first his view of reality is totally unknown to me. As I begin to catch a glimpse of it, it seems strange; it makes no sense; it may even revolt me. At that point I am sorely tempted to impatience. I want to tell him about my saviour, about the way in which Christ has been the answer to my very English questions, has set me free from my western temptations and fears, has proved himself Lord of our kind of family, and our kind of culture. If I persist and dominate, I may--once in a blue moon--get this other man to adopt my Lord, to repent of his sins, to pay lip service to my ideas of right and wrong. But his own real world, at the place where he feels deeply and reacts instinctively, will remain untouched.
>
> But if I persevere in listening openly I shall begin to see more of that other man's real world. ... And then, at last, I shall see the Saviour and Lord of that world, my Lord Jesus, and yet not as I have known him... the unique Lord and Saviour of all possible worlds (1972:189).

Contextualization in missions refers to a methodological approach. It should be grounded in Biblical precedents and be faithful to Christian doctrine, but it is not the doctrine itself. It is only a choice of methods to help reach various cultures with the Gospel. Its purpose is to make the Gospel clear to those who hear the message. The method does not exist for its own sake.

There may be a great variety of methods in contextualization, and tolerance should be displayed among Christians who choose different methods. Some methods may be more daring than others. Some may be open to greater success or greater dangers, and all should be open to review by both those inside a particular work and outside it. Methods will change, but the Gospel remains the same. Throughout the process love must dominate all attitudes, love for both those we are trying to reach with the Gospel and love for variety within the church family.

As long as a method does not violate Biblical doctrine or morality, and seeks the most loving way to adequately reach a people, it should be given a chance. If a method violates morality, for example, because it is founded on Christians bearing false witness as to the teachings and practices of those in another religious tradition, then that method should be rejected. Or if the method accommodates itself to a specific sin such as adultery, as in the practice of some Hindu Tantric sexual rituals, then that method must be rejected. But where the method seeks to remain faithful to Biblical principles, tolerance of different approaches must exist.

Religious Beliefs of Muslims

I would now like to present some tentative reflections on the concept of contextualization in ministry among Muslim people. We cannot talk about Muslim culture in the singular. Muslims make up about one-fifth of the world's population, and they live in numerous cultures with a diversity of languages and customs. Some have mixed folk religion with Islam, some claim to be Muslim but know little about their faith, and still others see themselves as defenders of purity in religion. Yet even within this great variety of humanity we can still find a basic Muslim context. They all claim to belong to the worldwide Muslim *ummah*, community.

The first step is to identify the parameters of Muslim belief. Doctrinal principles would usually be listed as faith in Allah, His angels, His books, His messengers, the Day of Judgment and the Hereafter. A Christian working among Muslims needs to determine how this basic framework of faith helps or hinders a presentation of the Gospel.

Concerning Faith in Allah[2]

The word *Allah* means "the God." Arabic speaking Christians also use this name. The Qur'an--the religious book followed by Muslims and made up of 114 *surahs*, "chapters"--says that Allah is the Creator and Sustainer of heaven and earth, that nothing exists or will exist apart from His will. He is the God of Abraham, Isaac and Jacob (Surah 6:83-84) and the various Biblical prophets. He is the God who caused Jesus to be born of the virgin Mary as a sign for all peoples (19:17-21; 21:91).

Some Christians may think that no one can know God or worship God if they are not Christians. I would suggest that on a basic level the people of the world "knew God" (Rom 1:21), and they even "know God's righteous decree" (Rom 1:32). According to the eternal Gospel (Rev 14:6-7), all people are expected to fear God and give Him glory--in other words, worship Him. This is a fundamental responsibility of all people whether they are Christian or not. We are not saved because we worship. We are saved by God's grace, and that is explained in the Gospel of Jesus Christ. But throughout human history, it has been and still is the responsibility of all people to worship God whether they are saved or not, simply because God is God. Muslims are reminded in the Qur'an to worship Allah alone, because He will judge us on the Last Day.

The Qur'an tells Muslims not to argue with Christians as to whether we worship the same God or different gods, but simply say to Christians, "Our God and your God is One; and it is to Him we bow" (29:46). Muslims reject all forms of idolatry. *Shirk*, the Arabic term which means to associate partners with God, is the most terrible of sins and must be avoided at all costs. For the remainder of the article I will use the term Allah for God in most places.

The Muslims' concept of Allah as it relates to presenting the Gospel offers special opportunities as well as difficulties. We do not have to convince them of only one God. They already affirm this and wish to defend the indivisible oneness of Allah against any concept of secondary deities. But they are afraid that we worship Jesus as a second god and are therefore guilty of *shirk*.

In our presentation of the Gospel we must affirm that we worship only one God, not two or three. Paul wrote, "God was reconciling the world to Himself in Christ" (2 Co 5:19). We did not make Jesus into a second god, but according to the Gospel Allah chose to reveal Himself to us through Jesus; He is Allah's self-disclosure (Jn 14:7-11).

Muslims believe Allah's word is eternal and yet appears in time and space as scripture. Jesus is called "His (Allah's) word which He bestowed on Mary" in the Qur'an (4:171). Muslims usually interpret this to mean that Jesus was created by Allah speaking the word "Be," and the virgin Mary conceived Jesus. So they usually think only in terms of this meaning that Jesus was formed by Allah's word. But the Arabic text refers to Jesus as Allah's word itself, which would be the uncreated speech of Allah.

In every other instance of creation there would be a distinction between Allah's creative word, and the thing it creates. For example, when Allah said, "Let there be light," the light is never called Allah's word. Allah's word is separate from the result, except in the case of Jesus who is called Allah's word itself; the word takes on flesh to dwell among us (Jn 1:1-5). And so Jesus' life in the Gospels reveals Allah to us, as well as the words he speaks prophetically.

Concerning Faith in Allah's Angels

Angels are not to be worshiped, because they are creations. The most important of the archangels for Muslims would be Jibril (Gabriel), because it is believed that he delivered the Qur'an to Muhammad between 610 and 632 A.D. They believe that two angels are appointed to each person, one to record good deeds and the other to record evil deeds. Some angels protect people from disaster. At death, two angels question the one in the grave, and the answers given cause a degree of bliss or pain before the resurrection. Most of the ideas about angels are later developments rather than Qur'anic.

Muslims also believe there is a Satan, but usually he is said to be a *jinn* rather than a fallen angel. Jinn are creatures made from fire who may choose to do good or evil. Some jinn cause much mischief among humans, and so various folk practices have become popular in different countries to protect people from these evil spirits.

In many parts of the world Muslims devote much energy to protect themselves from magical curses, the evil eye or jinn. They may wear amulets for protection. Some will write verses of the Qur'an on a slate, wash it and then drink the water for healing. Others will visit tombs of saints so that blessing, *baraka*, will rub off on them. Although many such practices may be condemned by some Muslim leaders, people still try them because of fear of Satan and evil spirits and a desire to keep away bad luck. Spiritual causes for everyday troubles are readily admitted.

Christians need to show how we can be protected from the powers of evil spirits by the power of the Gospel. We need to let Muslims know that the Holy Spirit of Allah can come to live in their lives. Since their deeds are written in a book (Rev 20:12), they need the power of Allah's Spirit within them to help them do what is right. They also need to know that Allah's Spirit gives them strength against attacks from Satan and the jinn, because "the one who is in you is greater than the one who is in the world" (1 Jn 4:4).

Concerning Faith in His Books

Muslims believe that Allah's eternal speech in the heavens is the source from which scripture comes. This source is called *Umm al-Kitab*, the "Mother of the Books." They believe that Allah has sent various books to prophets, and that in their uncorrupted forms these books all taught essentially the same message. That is: there is only one God who must be worshiped and served for His sake alone, because we must stand before Him on the Day of Judgment to give an account of our deeds. The Qur'an makes special reference to the *Taurat*, the Law of Moses, to the *Zabur*, the Psalms of David, to the *Injil*, the Gospel of Jesus, and to the *Qur'an*, the Recitation, as books from Allah.

Although Muslims affirm the Law of Moses, Psalms and the Gospel as books from Allah, they do not readily turn to the Bible for two reasons. First, they believe the Bible has been so corrupted that it is impossible to rely on it. Second, they think the Qur'an replaces all previous scriptures.

The usual way Christians have responded to these charges has been to attack the reliability of the Qur'an. That angers Muslims, and then they attack the Bible using similar arguments. I would recommend a different approach, by beginning with what they already trust. I would ask them to study what the Qur'an itself teaches about the Gospel in particular and the Bible in general, especially 5:47 and 10:94.

Concerning Faith in His Prophets

. The Qur'an makes mention of numerous prophets found in the Bible. Among the most important prophets, Muslims would name Noah, Abraham, Moses, Jesus and Muhammad. Some prophets have brought books from Allah while others have only delivered verbal messages. Christians working in Muslim communities would do well to teach Bible stories about these great prophets, and include others like Joseph, Jonah and John the Baptist who are also mentioned in the Qur'an.

Muslims believe Jesus is a great prophet and the Messiah. The Qur'an teaches that he was born of the virgin Mary (3:47) and that he performed miracles. He created living birds from clay by Allah's permission, healed those born blind and the lepers, and even raised the dead by Allah's permission (3:49). Muslim tradition also teaches that Jesus was sinless, that he ascended to heaven and that he will return to earth to destroy the anti-Christ. But Muslims in general reject two basic teachings of the Gospel: the divinity of Jesus and his crucifixion for our sins. This is because the Qur'an appears to deny these teachings; however, how can that be if the Qur'an claims to confirm the Gospel rather than deny it (3:3; 5:48)?

It is true that the Qur'an denies that Jesus is the "Son of God," but it is only a rejection of the false doctrine that Allah had sex with a human, and an offspring was produced. Allah has no son, because He has no female partner (6:101). To state the problem simply, Muslims reject the "Son of God" for two reasons. First, it sounds too sexual (112:1-4). Second, they have difficulty understanding how Allah would enter time and space without being caught in it as a creation rather than remaining the Creator. We can agree with the Qur'anic denial of Jesus as "Son of God" in a physical sense, and still affirm it in the spiritual sense. We need to remind Muslims that this title for Jesus was not created by humans but was given by Allah Himself in the Gospel when he said, "This is my Son, whom I love; with him I am well pleased" (Mt 3:17).

It is also true that Surah 4:17 appears to deny that Jesus died on the cross; at least that is the way it is usually interpreted by Muslims. However, not all Muslims agree with this interpretation. The verse does not deny that Jesus died on the cross, although it is usually interpreted that way by both Muslims and Christians. It simply says that Allah was in charge of what happened to Jesus, not the Jews who tried to crucify him, an interpretation admitted by some Muslim commentators.

Concerning Faith in the Day of Judgment

Muslims affirm that we will all stand before the throne of Allah in Judgment. One of the most dramatic segments of the Qur'an is found in Surah 81. It is a description of the destruction of this world when we are gathered to give an account to Allah of our deeds. The Qur'an also speaks of a scale which will weigh our deeds on that final day (21:47).

Many Muslims like many Christians would say that they are saved by what they do. However, Islam really teaches that we are saved by Allah's grace and mercy, not by works. Works are important, but we can never be so good that we obligate Allah to send us to Paradise. Even the pages of good deeds on the scales are weighed through Allah's generosity. Reward, for example, is promised to one who is martyred in the cause of Allah (22:58-59), but that person may be cast into hell if he had impure motives, and only Allah really knows one's motives. Neither martyrdom, nor religious studies nor liberal giving will assure one of salvation.

Both Muslim and Christian theologies stress salvation by Allah's grace and mercy. The distinctive Christian element is assurance of grace because of Christ's work. That is why it is so important to share the Gospel with Muslims.

Concerning Faith in Predestination

The Arabic term for predestination, *taqdir*, refers to Allah measuring out or determining something. Allah is infinite in power and ability, but He measures out to us finite power and ability. Traditional theology affirms that Allah is the Creator of everything, including all results. Before the creation of the world Allah ordained all that has been, all that is, and all that will be, both good and evil. This includes what will happen to us on the Day of Judgment. If one is destined to go to Paradise, one will never end up in hell, and vice versa.

Some might ask why people are held accountable for their actions if Allah is the one who ordains everything. A common answer is that Allah does not hold people accountable for creating the act. He holds people accountable for choosing the act. That is called *acquisition*. They *acquire* accountability for their choices, even though Allah causes the act.

In contrast to traditionalists who emphasize predestination, many Muslims focus on free-will for social change and revival of religion. They would say that we have freedom of choice within the boundaries measured out to us from Allah's limitless power and ability. Two key terms from the Qur'an emphasize responsible choice and action. The first is khalifa, vicegerent, or one appointed by another. When Allah said about Adam, "I will create a vicegerent on earth" (2:30), He was talking about creating one who would exercise stewardship over the land (Gen 1:26-28).

The second term is jihad. Although often translated "holy war", it literally means to strive in the cause of Allah. Muslims are to prohibit the evil and command the good as they strive to do Allah's will. Christians who work among Muslims can affirm that we also believe in Allah's control over the events of human history, but that Allah calls us to make responsible choices as we work for justice and righteousness.

Concerning Faith in the Hereafter

Muslims believe there will be a resurrection of the body for both the righteous and the wicked, and that we will all stand before the throne of Allah to be judged. Muslims believe that some will be sent to Paradise to enjoy eternally the rewards of Allah. It is most usually described as a beautiful oasis garden. Although Muslims are forbidden to drink wine here on earth, in heaven they will be granted "rivers of wine, a joy to those who drink" (47:15). But far greater than all other pleasures is the expectation of seeing the face of Allah.

Muslims also believe that some will be sent to hell. They are divided as to whether a person who goes to hell will remain there forever or eventually be released. Some say that one's condemnation is eternal. Others say that monotheists will eventually be released from hell after they have suffered for their sins. They will be removed because of Allah's grace when Muhammad or some other prophet intercedes for them. Whether they stay in hell forever or only for a prescribed time, hell is most terrible, and all should want to avoid it.

Traditional Muslims believe that a bridge extends over hell. It is sharper than a sword and thinner than a hair. By Allah's decree some people's feet slip from the bridge and they plunge into the fire, but by Allah's generosity other people make it across and enter Paradise. It is a graphic picture of the inability of any to escape hell, except by Allah's grace and mercy.

Religious Practices of Muslims

Once a Christian is acquainted with basic Muslim doctrine, work can be done on placing the Christian message within this context. There is another contextual issue, however, which must not be overlooked. That is the area of religious practice. Religious people are usually bound together by common rituals which give them a sense of community. If people neglect these rituals, they may still be considered a part of the community, but if people reject these rituals they will be seen as outsiders and possibly enemies.

Muslims have five pillars, basic practices which the community is expected to follow. These are supposed to be minimal requirements, but in actual practice many Muslims may be lax in keeping them and still be called Muslim. The pillars are: 1) reciting that there is no god other than Allah, and that Muhammad is the messenger of Allah; 2) prescribed prayer five times a day; 3) giving alms; 4) fasting during the month of Ramadan; and 5) going on the pilgrimage to Mecca once in one's lifetime if possible.

Some fundamental rituals bind Christians around the world together, and they should always be practiced and honored, such as baptism in Christ, meeting on the first day of the week for corporate worship and teaching, the Lord's supper, prayer and singing. The Apostle Paul never neglected any of these although he also worshiped in the temple in Jerusalem following Jewish customs. Muslims who become disciples of Jesus should also be free to practice their rituals insofar as they do not conflict with the plain teachings of the Gospel.

It would be wrong for a disciple of Christ to follow Muslim practices just to win Muslims to the Gospel. That would be hypocrisy. According to the Qur'an, hypocrites are among the greatest sinners and the curse of God is upon them (63:4). In contrast to the hypocrite, the disciple of Christ already believes in Allah and should be willing to struggle for what is right, not for personal reward, but simply because it is the right thing to do.

Muslims have a code of law for all aspects of life both public and private, *shariah*, "the path." A Muslim is not saved from hell by obeying this code of law, but it serves as the guiding principle for what to do for Allah and how to operate within society. The Gospel has no code of law, except to love God above all else and your neighbor as yourself (Mt 22:34-40). Why did Jesus not give an extensive code to the church? After all, Moses gave one to the Jews. Part of the answer lies in the fact that the Gospel stresses salvation by grace rather than earning it by perfect obedience to the law.

But there must be more to the answer than that, because we still need numerous laws for social relations. I would suggest that Jesus did not give an extensive code of law, because he expected his church to be planted within numerous cultures which have their own codes. Part of the contextualization process must be to struggle with how a fellowship of Muslims who become disciples of Christ may continue to live within this Islamic context without being thought of as traitors who have abandoned all law and customs.

A contextualized church may not look at all like a traditional church in America. It may need to meet as small groups in homes rather than in a church building. Perhaps it should be centered around a fellowship meal. As a part of the meal, the Lord's Supper would be served. Many Muslim commentators say that the Lord's Supper is mentioned in Surah 5:114 of the Qur'an. In that verse it is called "a solemn festival." This festival was to be celebrated by Jesus' disciples until the end of time.

If a Muslim who is not a disciple of Christ comes into the meeting and asks what is happening, the others can say, "We are having a meal together and are talking about Allah and His goodness to us. Would you like to join us?" There is nothing I have found that is against shariah by having such meetings. Some governments or Muslim groups may still oppose it, but that will probably not happen in most places unless it is seen as a threat to Muslim society at large. Then these friends who meet around the table can pray for each other, study scripture together and enjoy each other's fellowship. They return to their homes committed to being better Muslims in the true sense of the word as people who "submit" to Allah. They continue to be witnesses within the community by careful word and by action to the great things Allah has done for them.

Conclusion

The term "Christianity" has sometimes been a stumbling block, keeping people from becoming disciples of Jesus Christ. Unfortunately, Christianity is not always Christ-like. As a result, the name "Christian" is often looked down upon by Muslims. Many Muslims identify Christians with loose morals and no prayer life. America is seen as a Christian nation, and therefore some think America's television shows and movies reflect Christianity. When Western business people or tourists travel to Muslim countries and dress immodesty, or drink alcohol, or seek out prostitutes, this helps create an image of what a Christian is. Christians need to be Christ-like, so that Muslims will say that they understand the sunnah, the pattern of action of Jesus in the lives of his disciples. When Muslims really see this and understand it, that will be contextualization.

Endnotes

[1] I realize that Paul was more directly led by the Holy Spirit in his apostolic ministry than we are today. Our use of other sources does not carry the authority of scripture, but still Paul set a useful precedent which can be followed as long as truth is measured by the standard of the Gospel.

[2] The English quotations from the Qur'an used in this article are taken from Ali, 1993. See bibliography.

9

MANY OF THEM BELIEVED

by Nangsar Sarip Morse

As soon as it was night, the brothers sent Paul and Silas away to Berea. On arriving there, they went to the Jewish synagogue. Now the Bereans were of more noble character than the Thessalonians, for they received the message with great eagerness and examined the Scriptures every day to see if what Paul said was true. Many of the Jews believed, as did also a number of prominent Greek women and many Greek men (Acts 17:10-12).

The unconcealed praise that is lavished upon the Berean Christians speaks volumes about a conversion process that can best be described as a people movement. Obviously, Luke is not necessarily alluding to the qualities of superiority or inferiority when he says that the Bereans were more noble than the Thessalonians. Rather, he is most likely expressing his open delight and approval of this effective way through which people can come to know the Lord.

A people movement to Christ is a spontaneous response to the gospel message that is propelled by a widespread desire for change. Most movements to Christ rise to the surface on a groundswell of unresolved issues. These issues are usually of a proportion and nature that demand a group decision. It happens whenever a people, as a group, arrive at a major crossroad in life, and they must choose together which fork they will take.

Group conversions can be triggered by any number of factors. Some may be touched off by physical matters, such as war, drought or famine. Other reasons may be psychological, such as a perceived threat from a known enemy, or the sense of being perpetually oppressed by others. Most group conversions or people movements are brought about by spiritual concerns, such as a lingering fear of evil spirits, or a profound desire to reconnect with the one true God. Whatever the catalyst, when conversion does begin to occur, it usually will spread unabated until the entire group has been thoroughly affected.

Conditions for Group Conversion

Luke's observations of the Bereans and their conversion experience is crucial for anyone wanting to make an accurate assessment of a people's readiness to embrace Christianity as a group. How people respond to the gospel during their initial encounter says much about what the outcome of the effort to evangelize them will look like. Receiving the message with great eagerness is the single most important indicator signaling a people's sincere desire to become followers of Christ.

This does not mean, however, that the gospel will not encounter any opposition. The initial response of any people to the Christian message is always mixed. There will be those who are supportive as well as those who will be openly opposed to the spread of Christianity. Nevertheless, a people group that is on the verge of becoming a people movement to Christ will display an eagerness that is both contagious and unstoppable.

As I think about my own people's movement to Christ, I can see a close correspondence to the characteristics that were attributed to the early Bereans. The Rawang people of Burma also received the gospel with great eagerness when they first heard the message of Christ. My father, Sarip Jung, used to regularly tell us exciting stories about how our people came to know the Lord. He said that when the Rawang first heard about Jesus, the Son of God, who came to earth to lead His people out of darkness, the elders in every village spent endless nights comparing and contrasting the biblical account with their own oral traditions.

I have always been amazed at the way God has made Himself known to every people group. People the world over seem to have some sort of knowledge about God. Most people also have a clear belief in a creator God who was the maker of all things. My own people's stories about creation and the origin of human life have sometimes caused me to wonder if my ancestors were given a front row seat at Creation.

Rawang folklore is rich in its depiction of the struggle between good and evil, and it is peopled with characters of epic proportions. Our oral history is dotted with landmarks and descriptions of important staging grounds. They have been designed to help us remember and trace our people's migration routes. We have an equally elaborate cosmology that has significantly shaped our worldview. The Rawang elders needed to know if this new story could be reconciled with their own understanding of the world and its beginning.

The Importance of Winning Over Leaders

The path to conversion which the Bereans chose to take clearly underscores the importance of facilitating roles which leaders have to assume if they are going to help people find answers to their deepest questions. In a people movement, conversion moves out of the individual domain and becomes a group process. The issues that demand a switch in one's allegiance are not of a personal nature, but are more of a collective concern.

In a culture where a single ear of corn gets divided up among the entire village during times of hardship, the concept of a personal salvation must take a temporary backseat. In most tribal cultures an important endeavor becomes an all or none proposition. The idea being that, "If we really are going to a promised land, then we are going there together." The swift and surefooted, as well as the weak and the lame, will all wait for each other at the water's edge before crossing over.

Such a decision-making process requires the input and participation of everyone. It especially needs guidance from the community's influential leaders. This is not to say that a people movement cannot launch itself without everyone being on board. Actually, every people movement has in fact had to start off on wobbly legs. But as a movement gains momentum, it should have the backing of the group's leadership core. While there will always be spoilers who hold out, group consensus is what moves a decision along. Indeed, this was how the Rawang movement to Christ also unfolded. During the initial stages of the movement, some of the village leaders were unsure about this new hope that was being talked about. As a result, some decided to oppose the fledgling Christians, and many of the new believers had to endure persecution. In spite of this, the Christians did not become discouraged. They were able to see how God intervened in life to change the hearts of those who set themselves up against the gospel. Clearly, God was hard at work to make many captives from among the Rawang leaders.

The Role of Women in Conversion

It is interesting that Luke makes mention of certain prominent Greek women in his account of the conversion of the Bereans. There can be no doubt that in this passage, a keen observation can be made concerning the dynamics of group conversion. Along with the importance attached to a people group's having an eagerness to receive the gospel, and the need for them to secure the endorsement of their leaders, Luke points out yet another vital element--the crucial role that women have in the conversion process.

This observation about women and their role in group conversion has been amply borne out by the Rawang people's own experience. The rapid spread of Christianity among the Rawang people can be largely attributed to the enthusiastic and tireless efforts of the Rawang women. They were not only among the very first to embrace the Christian faith, but were also at the forefront in taking the good news from village to village.

Some major changes began to take place when the Rawang women started becoming Christians. In the Rawang cultural context the women had the responsibility of tending to the production of rice wine. This was an unenviable occupation as it not only involved hard work, but it also tied them to the task of serving up this potent brew at every family and village function. Rice wine was an indispensable part of Rawang social life.

Understandably, one of the first areas noticeably affected when the women became Christians was Rawang lifestyle. Suddenly, rice wine ceased to flow! The giving up of rice wine spread from household to household and from village to village. Within the span of a single year, rice wine had become a scarce commodity throughout the land.

The backlash from this was swift and furious. Rawang women came under severe attack from the male population. Many men took steps to banish their women from their own households. Many of the young people also came under heavy persecution for embracing Christianity.

The women responded by building their own houses at the edge of the village. This would then provoke the men to go and chop down the houses, which were built upon stilts. The men were then left with no choice but to reincorporate the women back into their families. These scenarios were repeated in practically every village until the women finally succeeded in bringing their menfolk kicking and screaming into the church.

As the primary care-givers within their societies, women are the most effective agents in promoting change. Because they are already accustomed to providing the best for their families, they are uniquely qualified to evaluate the merits of anything having worth. This has certainly been true in the case of the Rawang people. The Rawang women have made an inestimable contribution to the growth and stability of the Rawang churches through their genuine concern for others.

A Brief Profile of the Rawang People

The Rawang people belong to the Tibeto-Burman family of languages. Although they live primarily in the north of Burma, a few sub-dialect groups can also be found in China. Prior to their turning to Christ, the Rawang people were practitioners of an elaborate animistic belief system. They had a concept of the Creator, but lacked recourse to Him.

The Rawang are a group-oriented people who place great value in collective work. Long before the Marxist philosophy of collective work came into existence, the Rawang people were joining together in both village and inter-village projects with an impressive degree of cooperation. Working for, and safeguarding the common good of the group, was one of the cardinal values every Rawang subscribed to.

Long before they became Christians, the Rawang people had a highly developed ethical standard. Murder was practically non-existent among the Rawang, as they had come to attach great respect for all human life. Even the rare accidental death, such as would sometimes result from an inauspicious hunting trip, carried with it a severe penalty. Anyone who caused the death of another person, was obligated to pay a fine to the family of the deceased up to the ninth generation.

Rape was also something that was unheard of among the Rawang. Women were safe to travel anywhere without the slightest worry of molestation. Theft and robbery were extremely rare. People traveling to distant places could confidently leave food supplies at various intervals for use during their return journey. Food parcels were usually left at established campsites for everyone to see. Travelers never had to worry about others taking their food supply.

If someone discovered a honeycomb somewhere, but did not have the time to collect it right then, he or she could plant a stake in the ground to indicate the exact location of the hive. The person could then leave, knowing that they honey would be safe until he or she came back to collect it at the earliest convenience. This Rawang custom of marking things was so entrenched that no one would ever think of violating another person's right to something they had laid claim to. The practice could be used to mark anything else worth claiming.

This sense of integrity and uprightness is something that is common to many people groups, even prior to their encounter with Christianity. This is another confirmation of the fact that God has not left Himself without a witness among the world's diverse peoples (Acts 14:17). Indeed, God has revealed much of His will to those who would make the effort to learn His ways.

The Conversion of the Rawang

The Rawang people brought to their conversion experience a rich understanding of moral justice and spiritual awareness. Many of their cultural values and practices found deep correspondence with the Christian message that was being conveyed to them. Although the Rawang people lived in the tight grip of the powers of darkness, they had a profound knowledge of the Creator and knew instinctively that He was at the top of the hierarchy. All that they lacked was the knowledge by which they could be reconciled to God.

This knowledge of God's love was finally brought to us by our beloved missionaries. If they had not come to seek us out, and to share the good news of Jesus Christ with us, we would still be sitting in darkness to this day. For their coming we shall be eternally grateful. It was through their efforts that we came to realize the power of the Cross and the significance of Christ's resurrection. Their testimony and the life they modeled before us is what has continued to motivate my people to imitate their example in Christian service and outreach.

I am personally indebted to my mother-in-law, Betty Morse, for opening my eyes to the significance of our Rawang oral traditions. Her research into Rawang folklore and Rawang migration routes has done much to confirm the accuracy of our people's oral history. These oral accounts played an extremely important role in helping the Rawang people connect with the Bible's own record of redemptive history.

In the course of evangelizing the Rawang people, the missionaries were able to home in on many of the stories that were similar to the biblical accounts. For instance, the Rawang have a fascinating story of the universal flood which inundated the whole world. There is a story very similar to the Tower of Babel account where human language experienced its first breakdown.

There was also an old saying from the past which said that one day, people from a distant land would come to restore to the Rawang people the lost knowledge about God. There can be no doubt that these stories greatly helped to accelerate the spread of Christianity among us. It was as if God had already prepared the Rawang for their rendezvous with Him.

My father-in-law, Robert Morse, dedicated his life to translating the Bible into the Rawang language.   He became instrumental in uniting the Rawang people behind a common cause that was larger than their own estimation of themselves. With over seventy dialects to contend with, language usage has often been a sensitive issue among the Rawang sub-groups. Sometimes, petty differences and clan distinctions have gotten in the way of the common good, the very thing which the Rawang people have prided themselves as having in large measure.

The Bible translation work and literature production effort that has since emerged, has become the single most important force in providing the Rawang people with a genuine basis for group solidarity and purpose. This intense focus on God's Word has kept the Rawang people and their leaders rallied around a common cause. If the Rawang church is to survive beyond its birth and adolescence, it will need to continue maintaining this focus on the source of its strengths.

In addition to the Morse families, there was another family known as the Morrisons who served as missionaries among the Rawang. The Morrisons belonged to the Assemblies of God Church, while the Morses came from the Christian Churches/Churches of Christ. There was also a work among the Rawang by the Kachin Baptist Convention which resulted in the establishment of a number of churches.

These denominational distinctions, which have given rise to a number of persuasions, have without question contributed to the emergence of various distinctives and the unintended segmentation of the Rawang church. Could the evangelization of the Rawang people have been accomplished in a better way? Who can say? This was how God's sovereign grace unfolded for the Rawang. It is to the credit of the Rawang church leaders, however, that every effort has been made by them to actively promote and preserve the unity we have in Christ.

It is interesting to learn how the Rawang church leaders themselves have understood this configuration of Christian fellowships. They have tended to see it as a strength rather than as a weakness. One wise old elder explained it to me this way. He said, "Nangsar, it is pretty hard to cook a meal using a tripod with only one leg. You need the other two legs to make a complete tripod." He was referring to the standard iron-rimmed tripod which is a fireplace fixture in every home. What the elder meant was that each person's contribution is needed when preparing something that will benefit everyone.

The Day the Earth Buckled in Convulsion

By all accounts, the great earthquake of 1950 was the most effective instrument used by God to usher the Rawang people into His Kingdom. To hear the elders describe this cataclysmic event it to feel the end of the world rattle around in the middle of your head.

The swiftly advancing evening was imperceptibly erasing the last streaks of the magenta sunset that had filled the western sky with a breathtaking swath of color. In every community across the land villagers were preparing for the night by tending to their remaining chores. It was a pleasant time of the year. The late fall weather was crisp and invigorating. Most youngsters were out and about trying to get a bonfire or two going for the singing sessions that would follow.

Suddenly the earth pitched and jerked as if it was having a seizure. A deafening bleat, sounding like the grinding of a giant millstone rumbled down every ridge and valley. The buckling and swaying seemed like it would never end, as house after house was being pried loose from the ground. People who were caught inside their homes were tossed around like rag dolls in a box. Those who were outside found themselves bouncing up and down like rubber balls.

In an instant menacing black rain clouds appeared out of nowhere to hug the ground at tree level. While jagged flashes of lightning tore apart the pitch dark sky, claps of earsplitting thunder stunned all creation into submission. Hailstones the size of chicken eggs pounded the earth. A blood-mingled mud and slush began to flow freely. And still, the ground refused to stop moving.

Then, just as suddenly, everything stopped. A deathly silence enveloped the landscape. Not even a breeze dared to stir. Everyone remained in the position they found themselves in, dazed and exhausted. Slowly, people began to pick themselves up. They called out to one another to see if everyone was safe. Torches were lit, and family members attempted to regroup.

All through the night the frightening rumble of landslides could be heard in the distance, as entire mountains went crashing down into the valleys after being unhinged from their foundations. Surely, nothing could survive a night like this night.

So this was the end of the world. How amazing. How unbelievable! That was the thought that kept passing through the mind of every man, woman and child. The Christians must have gotten it right after all. They had mentioned that a day was coming when the heavens would disappear with a roar, the elements would be destroyed by fire, and the earth and everything in it would be laid bare.

When daylight finally broke through, it revealed a devastation that was mind-boggling. Virtually every river had been effectively plugged during the night as a result of the landslides, and lakes were starting to form as water began to back up in the valleys. There was evidence of massive destruction of fish and wildlife everywhere. The mountains looked like they had been mauled by an invisible predator.

The great spiritual awakening that swept through the Rawang following this harrowing experience helped to greatly accelerate the people movement to Christ. Without question, it was a sobering experience for everyone. The remaining obstacles to the spread of Christianity quickly evaporated as village after village turned to the Lord.

Spiritual Stretch Marks

The growth of all living organisms produces change and transformation. These changes often leave behind traces that tell interesting stories. Scientists have been able to read the history of the redwood forests through the tree rings of these denizens of the plant world.

The Church is also a living organism that undergoes continuous change and transformation. As the Body of Christ, it has a fascinating story to tell. Showing up in the fibers of this structure, the Rawang church is but one strand among many within the growth ring of God's own redwood giant, the Church. Yet even this thin strand has so much to convey.

Growth patterns record both the good years as well as the lean years. Nothing is really missed. Every growth spurt as well as every momentary arrest in growth has been recorded. All that remains for an observer to do is to come along and discover the design that has unfolded.

A number of significant emphases have been responsible for giving shape to the spiritual character of the Rawang church. These orientations have not all been of equal merit. Many of the distinguishing marks have been beautiful, but some have made the body look ugly and unattractive.

One distinct feature of the Rawang church has been its profound sensitivity towards sin. In the early days of the Rawang movement to Christ, Christians would openly confess their sins in church if they so much as happened to pick a flower on Sunday. This was not some mere routine the people went through just to be cute, but was prompted by a genuine sense of remorse that welled up from deep spiritual conviction. While this practice may seem bizarre to some of us today, for the Rawang Christians at least, it was the cultivation of a sensitive heart toward God.

Another characteristic feature of the Rawang church was its understanding and appreciation for the support of the church and its ministries. Rawang Christians have always been generous by virtue of their no excuses approach to Christian living. This has enabled them to not only take care of their own pastors and other church obligations, but to also be responsive to the numerous opportunities for cross-cultural outreach as well.

A persistent problem within the Rawang church has been its inability to establish functional parameters for developing an acceptable environment for the courtship process. Church leaders have tended to view as suspect any relationship that develops between people of the opposite sex. This has led to an inordinate amount of intervention that has spelled disaster for the very people the church leaders have so much concern for.

These examples, along with may other areas of struggle and challenge, constitute a group's spiritual stretch marks. Issues that are vital to the ongoing growth of the group must continually surface in order that they may be prayerfully dealt with. Scar tissue is never something to be ashamed of. It merely indicates that growth has taken place.

Maintaining Momentum

According to my father, the first Rawang to become a Christian was a man named Zarta Pung. He became a believer in December of 1917 while in the service of the British authorities. The following year he was instrumental in bringing his sister and five other Rawang families to the Lord. By 1925 a small congregation had been established in the northern administrative town of Nogmung.

The two decades between 1925-1944 saw only sporadic advances to the gospel among the Rawang. The period between 1945-1964 was the high-water years for the Rawang during which an entire people turned to the Lord as a group. The years between 1965-1984 found the church experiencing much hardship and spiritual weakness as Burma became embroiled in civil unrest. The period between 1985-1994 has continued to see the church experiencing dislocation as the country undergoes yet another round of upheaval.

If the Rawang churches are to regain the blessings they enjoyed during their golden years between 1945-1964, then they will need to return to their first love. At that time the Rawang Christians could boast of having an inexpressible love for their Savior and His Word. It was a time of basking in the sunshine of God's favor. It was during this same period that the core of today's church leaders received their training through the numerous short term Bible schools that were conducted yearly. Like the Bereans, the Rawang cultivated an intense desire for God and His righteousness.

Concern for Revitalization

The Rawang people have come a long way since those early days when the Christian message was fresh and their faith almost palpable. How times have changed! Where has innocence led to? The world has been too successful in muscling its way into the lives of Christians the world over. No longer is it a question of choosing between two masters; now it has become a question of which of the dozen task masters to serve first.

We have seen that the path to group conversion begins as a collective undertaking. The road to apostasy, however, always follows an individual decision. The long slide back into the mud-pit starts when we lose a single toehold. Today, the Rawang church stands at a new crossroad. This one is a major interchange. How will the church go forward? Will it take the subway or the skytram? There are so many modes of transportation to pick from, and they all promise to take us into the 21st century at warp speed. What shall we take?

Satan is still the father of all lies. Everywhere one looks, Christians are being challenged to rethink their values, to let down their guard. He still is the unrepentant thief, the murderer from the beginning of time, and he is determined to kill and destroy everything that belongs to God. Our enemy's favorite tactic has been to disrupt the family structure. Rawang Christians can expect to be shaken to the core in this area as well if they pursue what this world considers to be precious.

These are the concerns that are on my heart. Is it possible to lose everything we have gained within one generation? After coming so far in the Lord, are we in danger of losing our way? What is the distance between darkness and light? This is the great risk that accompanies all people movements. The intervening years can so easily erase from the collective memory the feeling of what it was like to be outside the grace and mercy of God.

This is why it is so important for us to continuously fan into flame the gift God has given us. The faith of our fathers must be successfully passed on from one generation to the next. This too must be a collective task. May the Lord find us faithful, and may He Himself safeguard the deposit which He has given not only to the Rawang people, but to all peoples who have come to Christ through group conversion.

10

PREACHING TO PAGANS: AMBIGUITY AND CLARITY

by Frederick W. Norris

While Paul was waiting for them in Athens, he was greatly distressed to see that the city was full of idols. So he reasoned in the synagogue with the Jews and the God-fearing Greeks, as well as in the marketplace day by day with those who happened to be there. A group of Epicurean and Stoic philosophers began to dispute with him. Some of them asked, "What is this babbler trying to say?" Others remarked, "He seems to be advocating foreign gods." They said this because Paul was preaching the good news about Jesus and the resurrection. Then they took him and brought him to a meeting of the Areopagus, where they said to him, "May we know what this new teaching is that you are presenting? You are bringing some strange ideas to our ears, and we want to know what they mean." (All the Athenians and the foreigners who lived there spent their time doing nothing but talking about and listening to the latest ideas).

Paul then stood up in the meeting of the Areopagus and said, "Men of Athens! I see that in every way you are very religious. For as I walked around and looked carefully at your objects of worship, I even found an altar with this inscription: TO AN UNKNOWN GOD. Now what you worship as something unknown I am going to proclaim to you.

"The God who made the world and everything in it is the Lord of heaven and earth and does not live in temples built by hands, as if he needed anything, because he himself gives all men life and breath and everything else. From one man he made every nation of

men, that they should inhabit the whole earth; and he determined the times set for them and the exact places where they should live. God did this so that men would seek him and perhaps reach out for him and find him, though he is not far from each one of us. 'For in him we live and move and have our being.' As some of your own poets have said, 'We are his offspring.'

"Therefore since we are God's offspring, we should not think that the divine being is like gold or silver or stone—an image made by man's design and skill. In the past God overlooked such ignorance, but now he commands all people everywhere to repent. For he has set a day when he will judge the world with justice by the man he has appointed. He has given proof of this to all men by raising him from the dead."

When they heard about the resurrection of the dead, some of them sneered, but others said, "We want to hear you again on this subject." At that, Paul left the Council. A few men became followers of Paul and believed. Among them was Dionysius, a member of the Areopagus, also a woman named Damaris, and a number of others (Acts 17:16-34).

The Gospel Goes to the Gentiles

The book of Acts is so lively because it is filled with stories. In the early chapters the drama plays out within Palestine, but by chapter 11 we are whisked away to Antioch in the company of nameless people driven out of Jerusalem during the persecution of Stephen. Probably the most significant moment in the history of Christian missions receives only one line: "Some of them, however, men from Cyprus and Cyrene, went to Antioch and began to speak to Greeks also, telling them the good news about the Lord Jesus" (Acts 11:20).

We do not know who these people were. We don't know who left under the persecution surrounding Stephen, went to Phoenicia, Cyrene and Antioch, but spoke only to Jews. Our lack of knowledge in such cases is not as unusual as we might think. The church in the area of Rome was started by folks we have no names for, not even any descriptions. The church historians of the fifth century tell us tales of missionary enterprises undertaken by unnamed traders, slaves and captives. That is how the good news gets around.

The work in Tuebingen, Germany in which I was involved from 1972-1977 began because of a German named Ludwig von Gerdtell who opposed Hitler, eventually had to escape to America and ended up teaching at Butler School of Religion in Indianapolis. His own life story was riveting because he escaped the Gestapo with only a few minutes to spare, minutes given to him by a friend at the telegraph office who did not deliver the order for his arrest until he had let von Gerdtell know. The secret police searched the next train leaving town, but they were certain von Gerdtell would hide in the open seating of second or third class compartments. Instead Ludwig sat in first class, dressed in top hat and tails. He got away because the Gestapo never thought he would be so brazen.

But the movement in eastern Germany which von Gerdtell led was itself made up of nameless folks who resisted both the ruling culture of Germany of the ate 1930s and criticized the churches of Germany who succumbed to that culture. Most of those young people who hung on von Gerdtell's every word, thousands of them, are dead. What kind of lives did they lead? How many of their children and grandchildren are faithful Christians now having outlived not only the Nazis but also the Communists?

At Antioch, the early Christian groups who fled Jerusalem had a message to preach but we do not know much about what they said. We are supposed to understand how Christians spoke to Jews from the early chapters of Acts, including Stephen's speech, but we surely can surmise that some of them might not have pushed all of Stephen's points as hard as he did. Stoning discourages.

Those speaking to Hellenists in Antioch preached the Lord Jesus. That is important for three reasons. First, *kurios*, "Lord," was an old, accepted word within Judaism that was used often in the Greek Old Testament to talk about the one God. Jews frequently repeated the Shema, "The Lord our God, the Lord is one" (Deu 6:4). Jews who spoke Greek might have repeated this central text in Hebrew, but they would have known what the Greek was.

Second, calling Jesus "Lord" was a bold claim indeed. That kind of talk used a word of him that was deeply sunk in the worship of Yahweh, the one God. There certainly was no developed doctrine of the Trinity within Christian communities at this early period. But calling Jesus "Lord" demanded the beginnings of trinitarian thought. Paul would soon write 1 Co 8:6 in which he boldly takes Deu 6:4

apart and puts Jesus on a footing with God the Father (Wright 1991:45-58).

Third, *kurios* was a title given to Hellenistic gods like Zeus or Sarapis as well as important people within governmental and religious circles. Speaking to Hellenists about Jesus as Messiah would have been possible and may have been done. But by choosing *kurios*, these early missionaries could be true to the Jewish Scriptures, make the remarkable claim about who Jesus was, and speak through a word understood by their audience.[1]

How we wish we knew more about these refugees from persecution. When did those who talked with Hellenists decide that the gospel should be preached to Gentiles? Had they learned that in Palestine, or was it the shock of the urban metropolis that brought them the insight? Did they see something in Peter's visions that was more impressive to them than it was to Peter? After all, Peter learned to accept Gentiles in the faith but not in fellowship together with Jews in a single, local congregation (Gal 1-2).

Paul in Luke's Narrative

These nagging questions prepare us for the pleasure of the heroic stories about Paul. Those anecdotes give us so much more insight into mission among Gentiles. Paul enters Luke's narrative as a one who approved of Stephen's death, a persecutor of the church, someone who needs to be converted. He has his own conversion experience and spends time with Christians in Damascus and Jerusalem where he preaches to Jews that Jesus is the Christ, the Messiah (Acts 7:58-8:3; 9:1-30). But he rejoins the story, as a companion of Barnabas, precisely within the Antioch church. Indeed he undertakes his first ministry among pagans alongside those folk who preached the Lord Jesus to Greeks. For all we know, Paul would never have been the great apostle to Gentiles without Barnabas' invitation and that congregation's deep faith and practice.

Paul dominates Acts from chapter 11 onwards. The stories before and after the one in Athens show us what kind of person he is and how he preaches. Often he starts with Jews and then moves to Gentiles. When he speaks with pagans he can be forceful, even severe. At Lystra he and Barnabas are mistaken for Hermes and Zeus because they heal a lame man. Both of them tear their clothes and deny that they are gods. They know what the lines are and when not to step over them, who brings the Lystrans rain and crops, food and joy. Yet it is a struggle to keep the folk of that city from offering sacrifices to them as gods (Acts 14:8-18).

Paul also fights for the opportunity to take the Gospel to Gentiles, an allowance which the church in Jerusalem will not easily grant. They are growing well in Jewish soil; thousands will believe (Acts 6:1;9:31;21:20). They have no way of knowing that in little more than a decade their city will be flat on its back after Roman troops have plundered it. Only the leadership of the Spirit can move them to the underwriting of Gentile mission, the move that saved the Church. Had it stayed a Jewish group it would have had great difficulty making its way through the world without the city of its Messiah.

At the Areopagus in Athens

Paul's visit to Athens continues the story of his preaching the good news. It provides us with an interesting context and one of the longer speeches which Luke records. The narrative which sets up the speech is not too much different from what we might expect. Luke tells the tale with wonderful literary skill, particularly through the use of ambiguity and clarity. Paul is distressed that the city is pagan, filled with idols. We do not know if the one word Luke uses to describe Paul's reaction, *paroxuneto*, "distressed," means that Paul's deepest reaction is sorrow, rage or a burning desire to share the gospel. Probably all three (Bauer 1979:629). He reasons with Jews and God-fearing Greeks in the Jewish synagogue but he also carries on interesting discussions with Stoic and Epicurean philosophers. This incident suggests that in his early life Paul has been educated as a Jewish popular preacher and debater, one who is thus prepared to talk with the Greeks about philosophical and religious questions (Bornkamm 1971:6-12).

Paul does move easily among those circles. Later in Ephesus his friends do not want him to go into the stadium during the demonstration in favor of Artemis. It is too dangerous. But those friends are not only the Christians in the city; they are also pagan priests, the Asiarchs, who reside in that sacred center and evidently want to hear more from this learned and interesting fellow (Acts 19:23-31).

Therefore when Paul is disputing with the Stoic and Epicurean philosophers, he is not involved in odd discussions which he is ill-prepared to undertake. He knows how to speak with pagans; he mingles with their learned leaders. Luke describes the reactions of the Stoic and Epicurean philosophers in a much more straightforward way: "What is this babbler trying to say?" "He seems to be advocating foreign gods" (Acts 17:18).

These philosophers want to hear more from him, so they take him to the sacred Areopagus. But they think he doesn't know what he is talking about, maybe he believes in odd gods. His position, however, might be a new, fashionable discussion from which they could learn something--if nothing more than how to be up to date and prepared for the next wacky idea. They are free-thinkers, but they are also conservatives. Philosophers, yes, but they know some questions have been answered. The best religions are Greek; they have kept society intact for centuries. Foreign religions are barbaric with strange practices and strange ideas.

Luke moves back to Paul, once more with a sense of ambiguity. "Men of Athens! I see that in every way you are very religious" (Acts 17:22). Does the word *deisidaimonesterous*, "religious," mean that Paul is complementing them because they are deeply pious or is he demeaning them because they are so superstitious? Like Luke's description in vs. 16, we have no way to decide which of these options is the correct one. Probably both. Paul could be outraged at their idolatry and now berating them for their silly entanglement with earthly statues. We have information which says that those speaking in the Areopagus were warned not to be honey-tongued in their praise. Or he could be saddened by their idols and happy that there is a deep sense of religion in this sacred space called the Areopagus.

Luke's carefully-shaped story keeps you guessing, never letting you make a final decision no matter how many times you have read it. Read it once more with a group of friends and you might even think that Paul is angry at their idols, gets control of himself, looks for an opening to preach Christ and the resurrection, and uses their positive sense of religion and the statue to an unknown god as his entry point.

Cross-cultural work in Germany was odd because so often we felt as if most things were similar to our experiences in the United States. They just wore strange shoes and talked funny. Then we would see things that made us aware of how deep piety and superficial superstition were wound around each other in German culture. That entanglement made us sad, angry and eager to preach the Gospel.

We met many deeply religious folk who were impressive Christians. But some German practices were defeating. A pious German Catholic or Lutheran would take the season of Lent seriously: forty days to contemplate what the death and resurrection of Christ means. Forty days won't do it, but it can help. Yet *Fasching*, "carnival," celebrations just before Lent were the crudest festivals of the culture. National television broadcast scenes of great parties, with streamers, party hats and honored leaders so drunk they could hardly talk to interviewers. These drunken orgies are so much a part of German superstition that there are laws against bringing any paternity suits to court if impregnation occurred during *Fasching*. A deeply religious celebration has become an idolatrous carousal.

The Statue to the Unknown god

For Paul at Athens the statue to the unknown god provides a point of departure for his interests. The decision to use it is not totally dissimilar to the decision of the fleeing Jews who preached to Hellenists in Antioch. Preach Jesus as Lord, for the pagans have some sense of what "Lord" means. Point out the statue to the unknown god. Statues to unknown gods appeared in the ancient cities among very religious people who worried that they might have forgotten to honor some deity. At times when pestilence or plague broke out, they erected such idols with the hope that the unknown god who caused such disease might be appeased.

Paul uses that statue like a cup. What he wants his hearers to drink in is the truth about God, the maker of heaven and earth. His point is almost exactly the one made in the speech at Lystra, but here it is formed to attack pagan dependence on temples made by human hands and the service of God with human hands. The great temple, the Parthenon, is clearly visible on the Areopagus. And all those idols, made by human hands, stand round about. So Paul preaches the God not limited to temples, or the liturgies of worship, or the idols. This God needs nothing from human hands; indeed this God gives everything life. This God put people in different places at different times in order that they might reach out to him.

Again ambiguity and clarity. Would Paul see the idol to an unknown god as a part of the attempt by these Athenian Greeks to search after the most high, or does he use the idol to introduce his criticism of their temples, liturgies and idols? The answer is probably yes. This section of his speech once more has that rich, textured quality of classic literature. A Jew of Jews, Paul never brooks idolatry. It always rubs him the wrong way. He surely knows the critiques which the prophets made of Israelite idolatry, of their temple worship gone sour. Perhaps he also knows the incident of Jesus with the Samaritan woman when Jesus himself warned that worship of God was not tied to one local sacred place (Jn 4:4-26).

But he also shows a deep sense of apprehension for some of the things which these Athenians believe. They do reach out for God. In fact, some of their honored philosophers and poets speak two truths: "For in Him we live and move and have our very being," and "We are his offspring" (Acts 17:28). Here is a clarity which remains somewhat ambiguous to us because we are so far removed from the text. Paul knows that these two quotations are part of the mental furniture of his listeners, at least the Stoic and Epicurean philosophers. They will be pleased--if a bit startled--that this babbler who apparently speaks of alien gods honors some of the deep truths of their sages. At least he recognizes some truth within their accepted canons.

I doubt that here Paul employs some kinds of clever tactic which allows him to quote their philosopher and poets while deep down knowing that the sayings are false. For him these two sentences are true, truths uttered by pagan wisemen. That is clear. What is unclear is who first spoke these words? Aratus is often given credit for the first sentence,[2] but others seem to have also said something like that. It may have been a rather common proverb understood and recognized by a number of Paul's hearers.

Greek Truth in Christian Worship

The sentence, "For in Him we live and move and have our being" has in recent years been close to me because of its use at the funeral of my mother-in-law. She had been an extremely healthy woman who collapsed one evening while we were visiting her home. Her unconsciousness terrified all of us, especially her husband. The doctors discovered that she had an aneurysm in the brain, one they thought they could correct with surgery. But when they operated, they discovered that the ballooned section of the artery was too large to remove. They did another procedure and hoped it would help, but she only lived six more weeks before it burst. Those were six wonderful weeks, but she was gone. My wife and I had the awful shock of arriving late and finding no one at all at the hospital, only empty, disorienting death.

At the funeral, a beloved minister read a series of scriptural verses. I do not know whether he selected them himself or whether he read verses grouped together by someone else. But in that series of pastoral, consoling texts was "For in Him we live and move and have our being." That was the only phrase from this speech of Paul. And it was a sentence first spoken by a pagan philosopher in poetry. It was true when that Greek first said it; it was true when it became a proverbial saying; it was true when it came from the mouth of Paul and when that minister read it at the funeral. All true things are truths from God.

The Gospel Without Compromise

Paul continues his Athens speech, however, by noting some of the falsehoods of the religious signs surrounding him on the Areopagus. Precisely because we are God's offspring as your honored sages have said, we must not think that gold, silver or stone idols--made by human hands--are like the divine being. God has been patient with such activity in the past, but now God calls for repentance. There will be a set time of just judgment administered through one man, the one whom God has appointed and demonstrated to be the judge by raising him from the dead.

Clarity. Even in the midst of the Areopagus with its temples, idols and true sayings, Paul does not fudge the gospel. Idolaters must repent, for God will no longer overlook their ignorance. Judgment is coming through the just judge Jesus Christ, whom God has raised from the dead.

Having dealt with Sadducees who denied resurrection, Paul is prepared for opposition to that sense of reality. He probably knows from other contacts that some Greeks think of resurrection as resuscitated, but still rotting, bodies. Yet he pushes on with what he knows to be true. Perhaps his speech is interrupted because of a clear reaction to talk of resurrection. Clearly revelation to him; clearly vulgar nonsense to them. He doubtless wants to talk further and explain what kind of resurrection he means so that his hearers will not misunderstand the reality through their own sense of what it signifies. But all he does is mention resurrection and some sneer. How disruptive sneers can be.

Just as he acknowledges the truth of pagan sages, so also he acknowledges the truth of God's revelation in Jesus Christ. And although only a few believe there are some: Dionysius, a member of the Areopagus, a woman named Damaris, and others. The results are ambiguous. Telling the truth with love, even a tough love that calls for repentance, has its effects, but often not the ones we wish. Dionysius in the history of the church becomes an honored figure through a fifth or sixth-century set of texts on spirituality which carries his name and was quite influential during the Middle Ages.[3] He did not write the pieces, but the memory of Paul's intrusion into the Areopagus has had continued force through those works themselves.

Truth in Pagan Religion

Ambiguity and clarity. Clarity remains. Luke's great story of Paul in Athens calls a spade a spade. He is no thorough relativist, no unfettered syncretist. He preaches Christ dead and resurrected, judge of the nations. He also acknowledges part of the truth in Greek religion: two sentences from their sages. That is as clear as the resurrection of Jesus. For the present day Christian, there should always be an expectation that God leaves his footprints in the religions foreign to Christian faith (Norris 1984:55-69). No religious people is totally wrong. We must not forego preaching Christ because this is a religiously pluralistic world. But neither may we assume that nothing others say is true.

Ambiguity remains. We cannot always tell who is the author of some truth in another religion. We may just have to let it be. More importantly we do not know which of the various motives will drive us on a particular occasion or which strategies will be the most effective. When we see pagan idolatry, whether it is temples in Thailand or bank accounts in America, should we feel sorrow, or anger, or the burden of preaching salvation?

Yes we should. Which of those reactions should be the strongest is impossible for us to know until we are in the situation and praying for the guidance of the Spirit. When we look closely at the communities of other faiths, whether secular or religious, will we see sensitive commitment or superficial superstition? Yes we will. And which ways may we discern and accept the true while finding and rejecting the false will not be clear to us without study, meditation, prayer and deep involvement with those people.

Luke's story of Paul on Areopagus is grand. But grander still is the careful way in which both its ambiguity and its clarity guide us toward our own encounters with contemporary pagans.

Endnotes

[1] Andrew Walls pointed out much of this in a course on the relationship of missions and church history held at the Overseas Ministries Study Center in December, 1993.

[2] John Chrysostom, the great preacher who was eventually bishop of Constantinople, claimed in his homilies on Acts that it was Aratus.

[3] Pseudo-Dionysius, *The Divine Names*, *The Celestial Hierarchy*, *The Ecclesiastical Hierarchy* and *Mystical Theology*.

11

HOLDING DOWN TWO JOBS

by Doug Priest Jr.

After this, Paul left Athens and went to Corinth. There he met a Jew named Acquila, a native of Pontus, who had recently come from Italy with his wife Priscilla, because Clauäius had ordered all the Jews to leave Rome. Paul went to see them, and because he was a tentmaker as they were, he stayed and worked with them. Every Sabbath he reasoned in the synagogue, trying to persuade the Jews and Greeks (Acts 18:1-4).

As a youngster I enjoyed camping. Something about getting away from the city appealed to me. Our Boy Scout troop went on trips yearly to the mountains, and as a youth minister I took the church youth on various camp-outs. Later in Africa as a missionary I made many survey trips in which we camped out in between our destinations. Part of camping involved setting up the tent, and then later taking it down before returning home.

The tents that I slept in during those excursions were invariably made from either canvas or nylon so it was natural that I assumed all tents were made out of cloth. Therefore a tentmaker, I thought, was one who could just as easily be called a tailor. Instead of sewing clothes, a tentmaker sewed pieces of cloth together to make a tent.

In Acts 18:3 we read that Paul was a tentmaker. The Greek word used is a compound word, *skenopoioi*, which occurs in no other Biblical text. The term, *skeno*, means "tent" and the term, *poioi*, means "maker." In Paul's time a special sort of cloth, *cilicium*, was made from goat hair. It took its name from the area where it was made, Cilicia, and since this is where Paul lived as a youngster it is often assumed that Paul worked with this cloth to make tents.

But in fact the tents of antiquity were not made from cloth. They were made from leather. The tents were not permanent dwellings, but temporary accommodations. Related words in English that come from the Bible using this same term, skeno, are shrine, tabernacle, and covering (Friedrich 1971:368). It is more appropriate to call Paul a leather-worker than it is to call him a tentmaker.

Living among the Maasai of East Africa gave me an appreciation for leather working. The Maasai are a pastoral people with herds of cattle, sheep and goats. Many of the materials they use in their daily lives come from the leather of their herds: straps, coverings, dust pans, ritual clothing, belts, purses, sheaths and much more. The animal hides are scraped and pegged out to dry. Then they are cut into the various shapes and sizes as needed. Since the Maasai leather is not tanned, the products are not soft and pliable.

The Maasai use cow leather hides to construct temporary dwellings. These dwellings, which are really just pieces of leather put on top of interwoven branches, allow the people to have shelter without going to the trouble of building a more permanent dwelling. From these East African pastoralists, I was able to see firsthand how Paul could be a tentmaker using leather to make his tents.

Paul and His Trade

The Cilicia of Paul's youth was known for its leather goods as well as its cloth. Perhaps Paul's father was a leather worker who taught the craft to his son. It is not unreasonable to assume that Paul served a leather working apprenticeship before engaging in his rabbinical studies under Gamaliel. Since rabbinical students were supposed to have a trade with which they could support themselves, Paul may have engaged in some leather working during his student days.

Only two tools are required for working with leather: knives and awls. The knives are used to cut and shape the leather and the awls are used for sewing the assorted pieces together. The limited number of tools would make tentmaking an easily transportable trade--one simply took one's tools on to the next workplace. This is of course what Paul did later in life, moving between his stopping-points at Corinth, Ephesus and Thessalonica.

The New Testament pictures Paul as a roving evangelist--the Apostle to the Gentiles. He was both Roman citizen and ordinary artisan. He was comfortable in both synagogue and marketplace, with common laborers as well as philosophers. He was a man with a message--a scholar--and the ancient world understood such a role.

Philosophers played an important role in the Greek and Roman worlds. Their wisdom was appreciated as they talked among themselves with attentive audiences. Hock says that there were four ways in which philosophers supported themselves: 1) through the charging of tuition fees; 2) taking board and room in the home of a benefactor or student; 3) begging; or 4) working to support themselves (1980:52-59). Paul's tentmaking puts him squarely in the final category. His salary would be used to help pay for his lodging, food and clothing. Being able to meet his own bills would not make Paul a burden to others.

This is not to suggest that either roving philosopher or tentmaking was a lucrative trade. Paul spoke of his being in want (2 Co 11:9; Phil 4:12). At times in his ministry Paul received help from groups of believers. Still, he was able to write, "I am not saying this because I am in need, for I have learned to be content whatever the circumstances" (Phil 4:11).

Being content in his work, however, did not make Paul immune from the disdain of the upper class. Nor should tentmaking be considered a simple occupation:

> Stigmatized as slavish, uneducated, and often useless, artisans, to judge from scattered references, were frequently reviled or abused, often victimized, seldom if ever invited to dinner, never accorded status... Paul's own statements accord well this general description. He too not only found his tentmaking to be exhausting and toilsome (1 Th 2:9)... but also perceived that in taking up his trade he had thereby enslaved himself (1 Co 9:9) and humiliated himself (2 Co 11:7). His trade also is to be seen as at least partially responsible for his being accorded no status (1 Co 4:10) and perhaps also as a cause of his being reviled (1 Co 4:12) (Hock 1980:36).

Paul balanced the vocations of evangelist and tentmaker. He used his tentmaking so that he could have the funds necessary to preach the Gospel all over the Roman Empire. We can imagine Paul in the workshop in the morning followed by an afternoon of preaching and teaching. Usually the leather-worker would sit at a workbench, and in the workshop other leather workers would be plying their trade. The two vocations even overlapped because Paul was the sort to use every opportunity for witness. Surely as he worked with the other leather workers, the zealous Paul spoke to them of the Good News of Jesus Christ. Customers would not be immune from his teaching since a leather working shop would be a quiet place.

In his letter writing Paul was not reticent about the mixing of his vocations. He was quick to note that his evangelistic activities were made possible by his leather working, and that all Christians should work (1 Co 9; 2 Co 11-12; Eph 4:28; Phil 4:10-18; 1 Th 2:9; 4:11; 2 Th 3:7-12). He defended his own tentmaking activity because it allowed him to be a fully self- supported worker. Paul was not opposed to Christians who serve as evangelists supporting themselves by their vocational activities.

On the other hand he was quick to point out Christian workers are justified in receiving full support from other Christians for their evangelistic activities (1 Co 9:7-12). A soldier receives wages--so should Christian workers. Just as an ox should not be muzzled as it tramples grain, neither should Christian workers be forbidden from feeding themselves by their work.

The reason Paul did not take salary for much of his life as an apostle was so that he might influence others to follow his example. As Wilson points out, even though as an apostle Paul "would have been justified in receiving support, (he) purposely chose to go without it in order not to hinder the spread of the gospel..." (1979:22). Yet there were times in his life as an apostle that Paul did receive the support due a Christian worker. He unashamedly accepted the aid of Christian sisters and brothers, most likely from the church at Philippi (2 Co 11:7-9; Phil 4:10,14-18). Wilson writes, "Paul was not so rigid in his policy of paying his own way by tentmaking work that he would not receive support from Christians who sincerely wanted to back his ministry" (1979:24).

The Apostle Paul was a bi-vocational missionary. He worked at both leather working and evangelism, without apology. His stamp of approval is upon those who work full time to support themselves as they pursue Christian activities. So too is his stamp of approval upon those who receive full support from other believers to meet their needs as is their due. And we may assume he would approve of those whose bi-vocationalism falls somewhere between these two extremes.

Bi-Vocational Missions Today

Missionaries today fall under one of three categories. Some cross-cultural evangelists are fully supported by churches and individuals so that they may live and minister in another country. Other missionaries receive full salary from an employer for fulfilling a secular job, such as a computer programmer with IBM working in Singapore. Lastly, some missionaries augment their secular income with mission support funds. Since the final two categories involve receiving salary from secular work, we call these workers bi-vocational missionaries.

Another common term for bi-vocational missionaries is tent-makers. I prefer not to use that term because the general perception is that a tent-maker is financially self-supported. Wilson's book on tentmaking highlights this perception:

> But the Scriptures say that there are two types of cross-cultural witnesses. The first are those who receive full support from churches. This is the way the Apostle Peter was supported. On the other hand, the Apostle Paul earned his own salary by making tents. Even today, cross-cultural witnesses or "missionaries" fall into these two categories. Some are funded by the contributions of fellow Christians, while others support themselves through various professions (Wilson 1979:15).

Bi-vocational missionaries can receive some of their support from those concerned with worldwide evangelism. They may have a stronger prayer, financial and accountability link with supporters back home than those whose funds come solely from their secular employment. Finally, the emphasis of the term "tentmaker" is on the job of making tents rather than including the work of ministry, whereas the term "bi-vocational" highlights the two vocations.

For many years missionaries have been sent out by their churches and mission agencies specializing in roles other than evangelism, church planting or training Christian leaders. Missionary nurses, doctors, teachers, business administrators, mechanics, and agricultural workers are not uncommon. What differentiates these missionary specialists from bi-vocational missionaries is that bi-vocational missionaries are employed by some institution other than the church or mission agency. Such institutions may be government ministries, foreign corporations, universities, private businesses or trans-national companies.

Benefits of Bi-Vocational Missions

Getting Into Closed Countries

With the breakup of the former Soviet Union, dozens of countries have become politically independent. Uzbekistan is one of these nations. Located in central Asia, and with a population of many Muslims in addition to Russians, the country has had little Christian influence this century. Soon after independence, an earthquake hit Uzbekistan causing much damage. Thousands of homes were lost. The United States wished to send some relief supplies to the devastated areas. However, the United States and Uzbekistan did not even have embassies or consulates in each other's countries.

The United States Agency for International Development (USAID) sought out a medical relief organization that was already working in Uzbekistan. The relief organization, staffed by compassionate Christians, was asked to oversee the relief efforts and distribute the needed aid. The relief agency with its medically trained personnel did such a good job that they were asked to continue functioning as an arm of the USAID in Uzbekistan. The medical personnel, by virtue of their bi-vocational nature, are able to have a lasting evangelistic impact in Uzbekistan, accomplishing something that traditional missionaries could not. It should be no surprise that the one asked to head the USAID's assistance program in Uzbekistan is herself a "missionary kid" and rightfully views this opportunity as a missionary venture.

Today's world is not the same as it was a few decades ago. When I went to Africa in 1978 and then again in 1984 I was welcomed as a missionary. But in many countries today, the welcome mat is no longer out for the traditional missionary. The traditional missionary is one who has received a Bible college or seminary degree and is well trained for the role of church-planter, evangelist or leadership trainer. Nowadays missionaries who have such training and degrees are finding that they are no longer allowed to enter many countries. They are told, "We don't need any more missionaries in our country. We have plenty of people who are capable of doing your job." Or perhaps the country is antipathetic towards Christianity, and the last thing they desire are Christian missionaries.

At the same time, these very countries are desirous of foreigners coming who can fill jobs that they do not have enough qualified citizens to fill. They want skilled workers who can assist them in meeting their economic and social goals. Bi-vocational workers are recognized in government documents as "something other than ministers or missionaries; and socially, though they openly admit to holding strong religious interests and convictions, they validate their presence in their host cultures through interests, skills, or products other than religion" (Hamilton 1987:8).

The shift towards globalization and development means that those individuals with the proper skills and credentials--by which is usually meant a secular degree and training in a profession other than the ministry--are welcome to what we have thought were "closed countries."

We really should do away with the term "closed country," because these countries are usually not closed at all. Only in our perception are they closed. While they are closed to the traditional missionary role, they are open to the bi-vocational missionary role. It is preferable to refer to such nations as "creative access" or "restricted access" countries.

Supplementing the Work of Other Missionaries

The plea of this article is that many will consider a career as bi-vocational missionaries. But this plea must not be seen as a call to do away with the traditional missionary role. Quite the contrary--traditional missionaries are still needed. Today's world provides plenty of opportunities for missionaries and the church must continue to send forth laborers. A good missionary strategy should be one which utilizes both traditional and bi-vocational missionaries.

Bi-vocational missionaries are "intended to supplement the efforts of traditional missionaries--and not replace them or to diminish the resources which support them" (Yamamori 1987:55-56). One of my acquaintances is a Taiwanese medical doctor whose training includes specialized studies in the United States. Through his training he became an expert in the study of AIDS prevention. One day over lunch he and his wife asked me whether I thought they should become traditional missionaries since they truly loved the Lord and wished to serve Him. My advice was that their background and training uniquely qualified them to be missionaries--in the "secular" medical field. Later I learned that he was offered a job by the government of Thailand to work in that country to promote AIDS awareness.

What an opportunity he has to make an impact on that country in the name of Christ. His work would surely supplement that of other missionaries in Thailand whose eternal goals are similar to his own. He accepted the job. Together with other Thailand missionaries, he presents the whole Gospel to the whole person.

Contact with a New Group of People

My experience echoes that of Hamilton, who writes, "Church supported missionaries generally have had a difficult time reaching out to the business, professional, government and scholarly segments of society. Their social roles limit their effectiveness among such people" (1987:13). One of the benefits of bi-vocational missions is that this group of people can be reached with the Gospel.

The mission I work with has had a ministry in a Southeast Asian country over fifteen years. During that time the focus of ministry has been upon the rural farming villages. Some thirty churches have been planted in small villages, and only one church in an urban area. At the same time this Muslim country has been undergoing both industrialization and urbanization. There has been a noticeable shift from an agrarian economy to an industrialized economy.

Sensing the change, we decided that we should initiate an urban work. Our first bi-vocational missionaries in this work have entered the country as English teachers. When asked their role, they respond, "We are teachers at the English institute." Such a reply gives them a unique status in this country which places a high value on its citizens learning the English language. As they teach their English courses they continually come into contact with the emerging leaders of the society. They have open invitations to visit in the homes of their students. Often they participate in local celebrations. It is a simple matter for them to form friendships through teaching English. As opportunities present themselves, they proclaim their faith. Because of this use of bi-vocational missionaries, our mission now has a chance to share the Gospel among a totally different segment of society than the farmers with whom we have worked to date. Now our missionaries share the Gospel with bank managers, university professors, psychiatrists, and even the head of the local immigration department.

If our missionaries would reply to the question, "What do you do in our country?" with the response, "We are missionaries," many conversations would be immediately terminated. In this Muslim country the word "missionary" is well known and missionaries are not welcome. There is open government pressure to severely limit the number of traditional missionaries allowed in the country. In ten short years the number of missionaries has decreased to only about 10% of the total of a decade ago.

This same country has opened its door to bi-vocational missionaries. Of course these people do not need to put on their visa forms that they are missionaries, because they are not, in the traditional sense. Rather, they state on their visas that their expertise is in other professions. One man who has been gathering data on various job opportunities in this country was told by government officials that if he knows some who are trained in tourism or forestry management, the government will be pleased to offer them jobs. Yet another man told me that if a person has a Bachelor's degree in English literature, he or she can be assured of a job in any major city in the country teaching in a university.

Misconceptions and Criticisms about Bi-Vocational Missions

Even though the use of one's vocation as a means of spreading the gospel goes back to the Apostle Paul, some criticisms have been leveled at the approach. Most commonly, it is said that bi-vocational workers must spend so much time on their job that they simply do not have the time or the energy to accomplish ministry-related objectives. While every situation, and every employer is different, this might be a valid criticism. Most employers require a forty-hour work week whether one works in Los Angeles, Lagos or Lisbon. For other employers, a forty-hour week is minimal, and they push their employees to add extra hours.

Bi-vocational missionaries who receive a portion of their support from churches and individuals might be able to work part time at their jobs in other cultures, thereby freeing themselves to spend more time in ministry. But even if only few hours are available, we believe that God will honor and bless those who serve Him. Regardless of profession, all of us need to learn to use our time wisely, as befitting our Lord.

Another criticism leveled against bi-vocational missionaries is that they are not equipped theologically to function as good missionaries. Once again, each field situation and each worker is different. Some situations do demand a seminary education; in others such an education separates the missionary from those having less education. Many bi-vocational workers have spent years in their churches--some have Bible college and even seminary degrees. It is wrong to generalize. To have a profession outside of the ministry does not mean that one is ill-equipped to serve the Lord. We still believe in the priesthood of all believers. God uses those who allow themselves to be used by Him.

A third criticism is that bi-vocational workers put a low priority on language and culture learning. While many foreigners do not learn the language of their hosts, many others do. Nor does being a traditional missionary automatically mean that one will learn the language. Those who do learn the language of their hosts are those who place a high priority on language acquisition, be they professional workers, students, missionaries or tourists.

Finally, bi-vocational missionaries are sometimes labeled as mavericks. Surely this is an over-simplification. I know many traditional missionaries who might readily be described as mavericks. "Maverickness" is a personality trait, and the correlation between such a characteristic and vocational choice might be difficult to document.

Implications for Mission Strategy

The movement towards the use of more and more bi-vocational missionaries throughout the world requires that we change some of our tried and true mission strategies. Three areas that come immediately to mind are research, training and recruitment.

Additional Research is Needed

The notion of using professionals to do mission work opens up entirely new ways of finding fields for service. Currently our procedures have us sending traditional missionaries to fields where they are invited by established churches or missions, and to new fields where they feel called by the Lord. Getting into new fields with traditional missionaries requires that the country opens its borders to such workers. Research is then undertaken to find the appropriate area of the country for ministry. The emphasis is primarily upon either geography or people groups.

Bi-vocational missionaries may also do research related to specific geographical areas or people groups. But more importantly, research needs to be done to answer the question, "Where is my profession needed?" The emphasis is on the professional vocation at least as much a specific people group.

In addition to reading the mission's literature highlighting unreached peoples of the world, bi-vocational missionaries need to read the want-ads, the employment section, and the career opportunities pages of the newspaper. They should scour their various trade's journals looking for jobs abroad and foreign placement. They may also check to see if their company has branches outside of the United States which need to import workers.

Mission agencies must also be involved in field research. They need to know the job market in the areas where they want to place missionaries. Their executives should make it a practice to consult the various governmental agencies to inquire which sorts of professions are needed to carry out government programs. Placing partially-supported workers with government sponsored projects may allow the bi-vocational missionaries more time for witness than would employment within the private sector.

The country where I live, Singapore, is an ultra-modern country with the very latest conveniences and gadgets. Every week I read in the newspaper about the need for highly trained computer programmers. The country is actively recruiting such people to plug into various industries. It is a simple matter for a good programmer to find a secure job in Singapore. In the church that I attend we have such a programmer. He worked for years with IBM making trips to Singapore with that company. When that company downsized a couple of years ago, this man came to Singapore on his own. Currently he is writing computer programs for the medical industry so that various hospital computers throughout the nation can "talk to one another." He shares his faith with his co-workers, is active in our church, participates in a cell group, and has made mission trips to nearby countries. His wife teaches children at our church, writes curriculum, and ministers in other ways. This couple does not require any missionary support from abroad. Instead, they make sizable financial contributions to missionary causes.

Cross-Disciplinary Training

Bi-vocational missionaries are those who have been trained in more than one discipline. They know their professions well, and they know their Bibles well. Wilson suggests that they need at least a year of Bible college or seminary training to augment their professional training (1979:104). Workers who venture overseas without a strong Biblical background will find their ministry effectiveness is limited. While they do not need a full four year degree in Bible studies, they do need some formal training.

In addition to Biblical studies, bi-vocational missionaries should take some courses that teach them how to appreciate and understand other cultures. If they can fit in a course on techniques in language learning, so much the better. Since they will be involved in cross-cultural communication, such courses are necessary.

In summary, we agree with Yamamori who suggests that before bi-vocational missionaries go to the field they need some training in the following six areas: 1) Biblical and theological studies; 2) cross-cultural training; 3) missiology; 4) developmental and global awareness; 5) spiritual growth which would normally include active participation in a local church; and 6) their professional skills (1987:79-780).

Recruiting Bi-Vocational Missionaries

The Bible college and seminary has proven to be fertile ground for missionary recruitment--particularly for the traditional missionary role. But the future bi-vocational missionaries needed in the world today are by and large not to be found at the Bible college. They learn their professions in the universities where they can achieve their medical, business, agricultural, scientific, humanities and liberal arts degrees. Recruiters must target universities and the campus ministries located there. They will need to work with Christian groups who are majoring in ministry on college campuses.

Conclusion

The Apostle Paul's training in both tent making and in theological studies prepared him to become the most well known missionary of all time. Before he embarked on his missionary journeys, the apprentice had mastered his trades. With leather working tools, apostolic experiences and the call of the Lord sustaining him, Paul set forth. Where he went, he stayed, sometimes years at a time. Once he arrived at his destination he developed lasting relationships with people who in turn became co-laborers in ministry.

Can Paul be our role model today? Indeed he can.

12

LEADERSHIP TRAINING LEADS TO CHURCH PLANTING

by Dennis Free

Paul entered the synagogue and spoke boldly there for three months, arguing persuasively about the kingdom of God. But some of them became obstinate; they refused to believe and publicly maligned the Way. So Paul left them. He took the disciples with him and had discussions daily in the lecture hall of Tyrannus. This went on for two years, so that all the Jews and Greeks who lived in the province of Asia heard the word of the Lord (Acts 19:8-10)

The Roman province of Asia was the major focus of Paul's third missionary journey. From his base in its principal city Ephesus he was able within three years to impact the entire province. Leadership development was the key element in his missionary strategy for Asia. This province was evangelized by a movement inspired by Paul's activity in Tyrannus' lecture hall. Training for any far sweeping church planting movement on a provincial or national scale needs some counterpart to Paul's daily discussions in Tyrannus' hall.

Ephesus as a Strategic Center

Luke gives a succinct picture of the Pauline team's Asian evangelization strategy. At the conclusion of the initial church planting efforts in Corinth, Paul, en route to Antioch of Syria, stopped off in Ephesus (Acts 18:18-21). It would seem that Ephesus had already been identified as the next strategic church planting center. Aquila and

Priscilla, Paul's partners in both tentmaking and church planting, were left to cultivate initial contacts in the city. Paul whet the appetite of the synagogue congregation with some brief gospel messages and set off to finish his business in Syria with the promise that he would return for more teaching during a longer stay.

By the time Apollos came to Ephesus, where his gospel understanding was illuminated by Priscilla and Aquila, a nucleus of the Asian church had already been gathered. The small group of believers which sent a letter of introduction for Apollos to Corinth consisted of migrant believers, perhaps their converts, and some who had been won by Paul's brief efforts. From this small beginning the evangelistic thrust into all of Asia would be launched when Paul returned to establish a base of operations in Ephesus.

Beginning in the Synagogue

Paul began his ministry in Ephesus in the synagogue as was his habit. He had followed this pattern in Pisidian Antioch (Acts 13:14); in Thessalonica (17:1); in Berea (17:10); in Athens (17:17); and in Corinth (18:4). Paul, it seems, always paused on the outskirts of any city he entered long enough to make use of the culturally appropriate functional substitute for our yellow pages and locate the address of the local Jewish synagogue. His first appointment was with the specially prepared hearers in the synagogues.

Why would the apostle to the Gentiles so invariably first preach in the Jewish synagogue of a given city? Hesselgrave suggests that Paul's primary concern in the synagogues may not have been the physical descendants of Abraham alone. "His target group, the Gentiles, was represented in the synagogues by the God-fearers, the devout, and the proselytes" (1980:173). Paul thus utilized what Hesselgrave calls "the doorway principle."

The violent reaction of the synagogue leadership to the gospel message was just as predictable as Paul's pattern of preaching first to their ready-made congregations. In Pisidian Antioch (13:50); in Thessalonica (17:5); in Berea (17:13); in Corinth (18:6) and eventually in Ephesus (19:9) the larger group of Jews rejected the message and threatened the messengers. Only in Athens was this pattern not repeated. Could it be that the philosophical bent of that city made even the synagogue leadership more tolerant? More likely Paul withdrew voluntarily before precipitating a serious reaction. Athens was not a strategically chosen city; Paul had taken temporary refuge here from violent Jewish persecution in Macedonia. Corinth was his operation center of choice for Achaia.

The Ephesian synagogue is notable for its toleration. It was three months before "some of them became obstinate and maligned the Way" (Acts 19:9). The more violent reaction in Thessalonica had required only three weeks (17:5). Once the inevitable opposition arose, the first phase of Paul's strategy was concluded. He had gathered as large a group of converts as possible from the synagogue community. From the outset his vision encompassed far more than the synagogue membership. Through the windows of the synagogue in Ephesus he looked out over the entire province of Asia. The gathered believers became the doorway through which he made his approach to the larger community.

Paul's "Commando Group"

The Pauline team did not have to regroup after the fiasco in the synagogue. They were ready to move on to phase two of their strategy. I suspect that alternate places of instruction had been considered long before the opposition reached its finale. Stephen Hsu notes that "Paul was following a strategy that was designed to lead to an increased number of evangelists, not just converts" (quoted in Hesselgrave 1980:175). The Gentile God-fearers and proselytes who had been converted to Christ in the synagogue ministry had ready access and entree to the Gentile population of Asia. It is just as true to say that Paul formed an evangelistic "commando group" as it is to speak of his having planted a congregation. These commandos were effective--in a short time the whole province of Asia heard the message (Acts 19:10).

Luke is a master of brevity. In less than a verse we move from a small rejected remnant thrown out of the Ephesian synagogue to the masses of Asia having heard the word of the Lord! This great chasm is bridged with a simple declaration: "Paul...had discussions daily in the lecture hall of Tyrannus... for two years" (Acts 19:9-10). Phase two of Paul's Asian strategy was powerfully implemented. He trained and dispatched the commando group he had gathered from the synagogue to reach the influential regional centers of Asia.

Into the Classroom

Modern day students of Paul long for a fuller understanding of the program and content of the daily discussions in the lecture hall of Tyrannus. The best glimpse we can get of the program used in this training program comes from the reading of the Western Text of the Book of Acts which states that Paul used the building from 11 AM until 4 PM each day. It is generally agreed that this amplified statement was not in the original text penned by Luke, but is nonetheless likely to be an accurate picture of what happened (Bruce 1988:366).

Tyrannus (or his tenant) probably delivered his lectures in the early morning. At eleven a.m. practically all public activity came to a stop in this part of the world. Lake and Cadbury note that "more people would be asleep at 1 p.m. than at 1 a.m." (quoted in Bruce 1988:366). This pattern of life made available an inexpensive facility for use in the middle of the day when interested students and tentmaking instructors would be free to join the discussions. Such a schedule also demanded elementary training in self-discipline and self-sacrifice. Such traits are not unimportant to "commandos" of any sort.

Paul's shift from the role of apologist-evangelist to that of professor is not absolute. There is nothing to make us assume that only believers were present during the discourses in Tyrannus' lecture hall. It seems that inquirers and perhaps those who desired to argue with Paul joined the audience.

Apprenticeship

Paul's basic methodology for leadership training can be summarized in one word: apprenticeship. He did not abandon that pattern for the time he had a semi-permanent campus in Ephesus. He spoke to Timothy about a body of material in which Timothy had been instructed "in the presence of many witnesses" (2 Ti 2:2). Thus it is likely that Paul's practice was to make his instruction for leadership development a laboratory course. He taught apologetics by dealing with objections as they were raised in the classroom. Such an approach would have been a real aid to any sleepy-heads present at the siesta time lectures.

Though Luke speaks of Paul visiting only two other Asian cities, churches were planted and grew in at least ten Asian cities:

Ephesus, Smyrna, Sardis, Pergamum, Thyatira, Philadelphia, Laodicea, Colosse, Hierapolis and Troas. There is reason to believe that all of these churches were established by Tyrannus-trained evangelists. Paul's strategy resulted in widespread church planting throughout the province, although he, as far as we know, never ventured inland. We know of more extensive church planting in Asia than in any other Roman province. All of it resulted from a professor whose vision extended far beyond the sleepy-heads in the back row to encompass the entire province. Strategically selected and trained church planting evangelists multiplied the apostle's efforts throughout the region.

Evidence indicates the evangelistic efforts in Asia may have proceeded in the following manner. Epaphras came to know and believe the gospel while living in Ephesus. After training he returned to preach in his hometown, Colosse, and in cities nearby (Co 1:7; 4:12). His ministry was a fulfillment of Paul's vision for all of Asia which had been effectively shared in the Ephesian lecture hall. In that hall Epaphras had learned from his master how to persuasively argue the truth of the gospel in a manner particularly appropriate to the Asian context. He was directly responsible for the planting of the church in Colosse, but Paul had a vital role in what was accomplished by this alumnus of the Tyrannus School. Former classmates of the Colossian pioneer similarly multiplied Paul's ministry in Philadelphia, Sardis, Pergamum and all the major centers of Asian society.

Paul's Asian Strategy

There are many reasons why establishing Bible colleges is no longer the most effective way of multiplying churches in isolated areas of the United States. Nonetheless, leaders of pioneer church planting efforts in cross cultural settings will do well to consider both elements of Paul's Asian strategy: 1) initiate evangelistic efforts among those who have the potential to serve as "doorways" to a broader group; and 2) provide for effective, thorough training of workers in a laboratory setting.

Our Western bent toward over-specialization can hinder the advance of the gospel. On the field, the use of church planters to give on-the-job training in church planting will be more effective than having a few designated church planters, who leave the training school totally in the hands of leadership development experts. Paul seemed to work on the premise that ministry skills are better "caught" than "taught." He did not abandon that philosophy during his tenure as President of the Tyrannus School of Evangelists.

Asked to provide titles or job descriptions for Paul, few would call him professor. The fact remains that his widest impact was felt in Asia where his effort emanated from the lecture hall. This understanding is a great comfort to one who reluctantly became a founder of an evangelist training school, which today has a campus, a staff and the demands of a growing budget.

Ministry Beginnings in Indonesia

The beginning of the ministry of the Christian Church missionaries in Indonesia was largely prompted by the great reports of a massive turning to Christ in the days following the failed Communist coup in 1965. Atheistic communism had totally failed and had been prohibited by law; former sympathizers were open to new ideas. They were not disposed to embrace the religion of the militant Moslems who had so enthusiastically participated in the slaughter and imprisonment of so many of their friends. Some claim that among the Javanese alone --Indonesia's largest ethnic group--two million professed faith in Christ between 1965 and 1971 (Willis 1977:xiii).

The first wave of missionaries from the Christian Churches in America came to Java, seeking the opportunity to participate in this great ingathering. Tragically by the time the initial team was on the field and ready to begin work, the peak period of receptivity was beginning to wane. These missionaries saw their job in terms of evangelism and church planting. Some wanted to contribute to this cause by producing materials or audio-visuals. No one expressed great interest in starting a Bible college or school of evangelism. The focus was on the great masses, especially in the Javanese villages, who were open to the gospel. Primary evangelism was the crying need of the hour.

In mid-1976 the Lord began to open some significant doors of opportunity in the mountain villages just outside the city of Salatiga. Family web relationships led us into another complex of villages on the slopes of Mt. Merapi near the town of Boyolali. The operative strategy, intentionally or otherwise, was built around missionaries and their resources. Missionaries were on the cutting edge of all church planting efforts. The missionary's presence was a two-edged sword: on the one hand it showed that people around the world were concerned for the salvation of the villages; on the other it often gave rise to unfulfilled visions of prosperity-by-association. In the midst of this the Lord worked: believers were gathered, churches were planted and began to grow. Leadership was largely provided either directly by the missionary, or was missionary-dependent (e.g. the missionary chauffeured volunteer workers from the city into villages to provide basic ministry leadership). When a missionary had to leave, temporarily or permanently, the villagers always asked, "Who will replace you?" By this, they meant, what missionary?

Quickly the missionary force was over-extended and expansion ground to a halt. Missionary visas, at that time, were not difficult to obtain, thus, it was tempting to think in terms of greater expansion as being dependent upon more and more foreign workers.

Government Restrictions Become a Reality

Reality therapy came in the form of restrictive government regulations. Visas became increasingly difficult to obtain and restrictions upon evangelism were put in place. It became clear that a given missionary's tenure was tentative and that the missionary community would not be welcome indefinitely.

The training of men and women to lead in the life and growth of their local village churches became a priority focus of the decreased missionary team. Small group discipling theory coupled with experimentation in theological education by extension provided the model for ministry to existing churches. Increasingly in the churches leaders emerged who with varying degrees of success could lead the normal activities of their local churches. They needed outside help when problems arose and they were either unwilling or unable to reproduce themselves as leaders. In some places evangelism limped along in the local villages but rarely was there outreach to other nearby communities.

New efforts were planned and initiated in areas free of the burdens of past mistakes. From the beginning an emerging leadership was encouraged and trained. The improvement was more of degree than nature. Some of them proved to be more concerned and faithful as spiritual leaders for their congregations but none were effective in initiating outreach efforts which resulted in churches being started.

By the mid 1980's a resurgence of Islamic identity was becoming increasingly apparent. This has resulted in greater barriers to gospel expansion in villages which were formerly wide open. The government encouraged program of widespread mosque construction elevated and sealed the Moslem self-image in many villages. Foreign religious workers were told that their stay would be limited and they must plan for Indonesianization. Visa renewals required work plans which specified what training was being done by the religious workers to equip an Indonesian citizen to replace the worker. Soon it was decreed that no foreign religious worker could remain in Indonesia more than ten years. These and other restrictive regulations were gradually set into motion over a period of four to five years.

A New Approach

In 1984 the Indonesian Christian Church Theological School was officially registered with the government. All workers who had formerly been registered as missionaries or church workers changed their registration to a new government encouraged designation, "expert in theology," and were assigned to teach in the newly established school. The official office of the school was established in the building of the church in Salatiga; more formal records were instigated; and certificate requirements were specified, but the content and purpose of our leadership training programs was unchanged. The results were generally the same.

In March 1987 all the governmental regulations became intensely personal for our family. We were told that our visas would be renewed for only one more year. We would be expected to leave Indonesia in March 1988. Threatened with a similar fate several years before, we had felt constrained to leave some written statement of the basic doctrine that had been taught in our churches. Two books of biblical doctrine had been translated and published in Indonesia. In 1987 we felt that such books in and of themselves would not be good enough. We determined to use whatever time the Lord would grant us in Indonesia to equip promising young people who would influence this nation for the Lord.

By then our missionary team in Central Java had already shrunk to three families and one single. The best information we had was that those missionaries would likely lose their visas at the rate of approximately one per year over the following three or four years. Our team's last new missionary visa had been granted more than seven years earlier. Our last opportunity to communicate the burden for and understanding of the expansion of church planting evangelism had arrived. We had one last chance to produce workers who had caught the vision and shared the commitment.

First Students

Our family was living in a relatively large village home which could be easily reworked to provide both classroom and sleeping space for several students. In July 1987 we added three young men to our family, and the campus program of the Indonesian Christian Church Theological School was born. We anticipated that it would be a one year program.

We lived, worked, prayed, and played together. In many ways we became an extended family. The demands of the discipling relationship were inescapable. There was no way to hide our manner of life. It was plainly visible. They quickly learned what we valued and what our weaknesses were. We lived in the middle of an area surrounded by both unevangelized villages and newly planted village congregations. The laboratory was at hand. Each morning we studied a different subject together and often in the afternoons and evenings we went out to do village evangelism together.

Joko was just beginning to recover from a very serious case of tuberculosis. He felt that every breath he took was a gift from God. He lived a life of gratitude and eagerly accepted the instruction which because of his disease had been denied him at a more formal program. During that first year he returned each week-end to his home village where he led a dozen people to faith in the Lord.

Martono was not old enough to gain acceptance into the school of his choice, so he came to live and study with us for a year. He has a clear, sharp mind and an eager inquisitive spirit. During that year together he led a team of two or three young people from the Salatiga city congregation into the village of Clowok each week. Their efforts were blessed with the firm establishment of a congregation of believers.

Petrus came not from Java but from Sulawesi. He found it more difficult to effectively communicate the gospel in Javanese villages, but a faithful servant spirit that has continued to this day became apparent.

The first serious exposure that these young men had to cross cultural communication of the gospel came in an unplanned manner. By some means that still remain a mystery to me, one at a time over a period of a few months several young men from the strongly Islamic island of Madura happened by our village house to ask for financial assistance. Each had left the rocky island just off the coast of East Java to look for work, and each was returning disappointed and broke. They needed money for bus fare.

We had been studying evangelism when one of these young Madurese stopped by. As I was talking with him I thought, "He needs more than a few coins." I called the three students in and asked them to share the gospel with the young man. As I expected, they found him quite resistant. In fact, we were all shocked by the level of his resistance. I invited the young man to share lunch with us before going on his way. One of us told him we would pray before we ate. He replied, "Kill me, but don't make me pray to your God."

This experience taught these evangelists-in-training much about evangelism, prayer and cross cultural communication. The experience as a teaching tool was worth much more than the fifty cents or so I shared with the young man to help with his bus fare. The encounter could not have been scheduled in a campus program.

If these students had not been living in our house, we would have missed other frequent opportunities to involve them in unplanned ministry events. In Java, for example, one is often given only a couple of hours warning to prepare for a funeral. Our informal format made it possible for us to quickly rearrange schedules and go off to minister together. If I were away and someone came from a village church with a problem or a need, you do not need to guess who got the experience of dealing with it.

That year was one of the most stressful of our missionary career. I was frequently on the road seeking information from various government offices trying to find a way to remain in Indonesia. It was a time of introspection when we learned that we could likely remain in Indonesia if I would apply for Indonesian citizenship. On the other hand, it was a time of unequaled joy as we rejoiced in deep personal fellowship with Indonesian brothers. Nothing has been as satisfying in ministry as to see the fruit develop in the evangelistic ministry of those we have trained. We first saw this in a significant way in the year that was supposed to be our last in Indonesia.

The only loosening of the governmental restrictions on missionary presence and activity in Indonesia since 1987 has been in the granting of a limited number of new visas which will be valid for only three years. Practical requirements coupled with the biblical example continues to make an emphasis upon leadership development imperative.

The Move to a Permanent Campus

We basically followed our "mom and pop" evangelist training model for three more years. Since 1991 we have had a permanent campus location. The challenges of meeting our basic goals are not unattainable but are more challenging from the campus location.

Since 1987 many new government requirements have been placed upon educational programs. Visas for foreign workers are now available only to programs that focus upon training at a post- secondary level. A formal campus is necessary, as is a clearly defined leadership structure. Even a standardized curriculum is being promoted. Totally yielding to either government regulations or to societal demands can detour us from the Tyrannus model. A determination to follow this model will continue to demand creativity and flexibility, but I am convinced will bear abiding fruit. The worthiness of the strategy directly corresponds to how well we follow the Pauline example: constantly focusing upon the target people through the lens of the students we are equipping in the classroom.

The real value of any training program, from a strategic standpoint, must be judged by its commitment to evangelism and church planting. Give us a classroom with even a small percentage of students who are the caliber of Epaphras, or Joko, or Martono and we will feel that our teaching is strategically important to the accomplishment of church planting goals. Give us a classroom of straight "A", degree-seeking theoretical students who are delaying involvement in evangelistic ministry, and frustration will promptly set in. The student should never be viewed as the end product. A church planting movement is a more worthy goal.

Paul's Strategy in an Indonesian Setting

In Luke's brief notes we do not have a definitive delineation of the philosophy or program of the Tyrannus School of Evangelists, but we do have a few insights into how Paul was able to effectively train workers who penetrated a whole province in two or three short years. We will now consider four of these insights against the backdrop of the current leadership training program with which we are working in Indonesia.

Preparation in Ministry

In Acts 19 and elsewhere we find Paul training workers in ministry, not merely for ministry. Paul's invitation for Timothy to join him and Silas in their travels is reminiscent of the Savior's call to "Follow Me" (Acts 16:3). For both Paul and Jesus the basic method of training began with involving the disciple in day-to-day ministry. We assume that Paul, as the Lord did, frequently set aside time to explain the reasons behind certain actions and the foundational truths upon which those actions were based.

Hesselgrave describes Paul's basic pattern of church planting evangelism in these words: "He engaged in evangelism himself, he trained others to do the same work, and he left others to do the work for which they had been trained" (1980:186). Good discipleship methodology always emphasizes at least four basic steps: 1) the trainer does a certain ministry while the trainee observes; 2) the trainer explains the course of action, answering specific questions from the trainee; 3) the trainee does the ministry with the trainer observing; and 4) follow up evaluation and encouragement are given to the trainee. Successful salespeople are often trained in ways very similar to those set forth here. It is reassuring to know that the pilot of an aircraft on which I am a passenger received training in a similar manner, not via a correspondence course.

When we move any instruction into a formal classroom setting, we are tempted to focus on the factual memorization of the theoretical elements of the problem. Practical application can too easily be left for a more convenient time. In such a program graduation day is often met with "Now what?" emotions. Graduation in such a program is accurately called commencement-- a time of beginning. Both Jesus and Paul gave basic ministry instruction in the midst of active personal ministries in which their disciples were immediately involved. Paul's lecture hall tenure was not a departure from this pattern. In all likelihood he welcomed the ignorant and the unconvinced into the lecture hall. His leadership development was via evangelism. While doing evangelism he was also instructing others in the principles and practices of evangelism.

In simpler days medical doctors and ministers of the gospel were trained in the apprentice system. A trainee attached himself to an older practitioner, traveled with him, questioned him about his actions and decisions, read his books, and gradually was given increased responsibility, especially after the inevitable crucial day when his trainer was not available to deal with a great crisis. At last the trainee could be dispatched to a needy area, or assume what had previously been the responsibility of his mentor. Recent emphasis on internships in theological education is an effort to regain some of what has been lost in the migration to the formal classroom.

Proven Instructors

Often it is felt that one can get the best medical treatment in a hospital that is attached to a medical school. There the best medical minds have been gathered to instruct the next generation of doctors. Careful medical instructors lead their charges among the patients showing--not merely telling--them how to properly diagnose and treat. This is a worthy model for the training of church planting evangelists. We must have a faculty who have proven themselves in the real life church planting "clinic." Professor Paul met that criteria. He had pioneered church planting movements in Cyprus, Galatia, Macedonia, Achaia and other places before becoming the temporary Honored Professor of Church Planting in Ephesus.

Once again Hesselgrave has clearly underscored this point. He stresses that courses in missions and evangelism will lack "concreteness" until they focus on devising strategies for church-extension evangelism in designated areas (1980:75). This "concreteness" and "specificity" for which Hesselgrave longs requires an instructor who has done more than read the second-hand evaluations of how others implemented their strategies. The professor should have been in the trenches in the not-too-distant past, and in a cultural setting not-too-far removed from the one at hand.

This becomes a challenge in a school such as the one with which we work. To secure a visa for Indonesia, a Christian worker with acceptable credentials must be invited to teach in a leadership development school. On the other hand, we are contending that if one is to be fully qualified to teach in such a school, he or she should have specific experience in church planting in that or a similar context. The best we can hope for is that a new teacher will focus teaching on areas of competence while being involved directly in church planting efforts where the necessary practical experience can be gained. The average Westerner in such a setting feels he or she is functioning inadequately in both tasks. Once again we come up against a dichotomy of roles which naturally flows from our western tendency toward over-specialization.

A number of theoreticians who on the basis of their deep study can call the practitioner's inefficiencies into account are invaluable and should be encouraged in their ministry. But training for the church expansion team is best done not by the theoretician but by the practitioner who can and will say, "Come with me." The source of our personal boldness in beginning a school for church planting evangelists was not our educational preparation (admittedly weak in several areas), but was the experience we had recently gained in a pioneer church planting effort in an area new to our churches.

There is a fly in the ointment however. Faced with today's glorification of specialization the humble practitioner rarely feels equipped to initiate formal training. It is unlikely that we personally would have taken that step had circumstances not nudged us in that direction. But we are under obligation to pass on to reliable people what we have received (2 Ti 2:2). The primary function of the pastor, teacher and evangelist is to equip the saints for their ministry (Eph 4:11-12).

Challenge to Commitment

I rather suspect that Professor Paul was deliberate in his selection of siesta time for his daily discussions. At that time people who really wanted to be there could. The half-hearted would simply not make the effort. Paul's commandos for the Asia invasion had to be willing to pay the price. Some would go into what was later likened to Satan's throne room--Pergamum. Some would face vicious opposition from those who falsely claimed to be descendants of Abraham. None were going on a picnic.

Taking Asia for Christ was no walk in the park. The commando force was trained in the shadow of Diana's temple, a symbol of pagan resistance to the things of God. Jesus had told his trainees, "I am sending you out like sheep among wolves" (Mt 10:16). Paul's Asia was no kinder than Jesus' Judea. Paul wrote to the saints in Corinth from Ephesus where he said he had "fought wild beasts" (1 Co 15:32). Later he evaluated the Asia challenge in these words, "A great door for effective work has opened to me, and there are many who oppose me" (1 Co 16:9). Those who would not sacrifice a siesta would be of no help in such a fight.

When I first began to think of committing my life to preaching and evangelism, the old gospel hymn, "Throw Out the Lifeline," expressed my commitment. People were drowning, therefore they needed (and would welcome, I thought) a rescue squad. When I arrived on the scene I found that the lost were being held captive in a fortress, protected by all sorts of vicious warriors, and that the captives for the most part had been brainwashed. I came to war armed with a rope and a life preserver! We have suffered many casualties among the casually prepared.

Paul restated much of his philosophy and teaching for Timothy in two letters which were delivered to him at his Ephesus address a decade or so later. "Endure hardship," he wrote, "like a good soldier of Christ Jesus" (2 Ti 2:3). Paul, knowing what the battle was like, would not be inclined to waste time trying to train the pampered and the spoiled.

Paul himself worked in the leather shop all morning, and then came to the lecture hall to conduct his priority business. This man who challenged others, "Follow me as I follow Christ", would not likely be inclined to invest much time or training in one who was not willing to adjust his lifestyle enough to study at what was universally agreed to be an inconvenient time.

The selection of students for any church planting training program must always stress the challenge to and the need for commitment. In an environment where one must often purchase a space in the university classroom, pay for passing grades, make an appropriate contribution to graduate, and then buy a job, it is a small wonder that some less-than-serious students are happy to go to a bible school where entrance is easy and the minimal fees are often underwritten by a sponsor.

On the other hand there are many worthy students like Joko. His widowed mother and family had no resources to pay even minimal fees for his training. Had it not been for the generosity of other

Christians his tuberculosis would have gone untreated and barring divine intervention he would be dead today. He did not opt to study because it was a quick way to a supposedly easy job. He both needed and was worthy of assistance.

While it is my conviction that an education is too valuable to be given to anyone gratis, the opportunity for part time employment is practically non-existent in Java. The challenge of how to help worthy students without overindulging them is one of the most demanding and persistent ones we face. We have been able to make some limited campus programs available. The purpose is to help students earn needed funds.

Student selection is almost as demanding as student training. Paul made it possible for his students to support themselves by working in the morning hours and then studying in their normal rest time. Only the determined would tackle the demands of such a schedule. We are praying for the same kinds of students and a culturally appropriate way for them to help support themselves.

Appropriate Curriculum

How I wish I had a catalogue from the Tyrannus School of Evangelists. We are left to look elsewhere for clues as to what specific training Paul gave his co-workers in church expansion evangelism. We do know that his commandos got what they needed. The proof is in the success of their efforts.

Hesselgrave argues effectively that Paul's church expansion team was given specialized training that differed from the training of the saints in a local church. He draws a parallel with the differing training Jesus gave the twelve and the multitudes (1980:151).

Timothy and Titus as young evangelists had been trained to articulate true doctrine and to recognize and oppose false teaching (Tit 2:1,10; 2 Ti 2:2; 3:10; 4:13). Titus had been equipped with at least basic accounting skills (2 Co 8:1-6,16-21). Both he and Timothy understood basic church administration (1 Ti 3:1-14; Tit 1:5-9). The importance of character formation had not been neglected in their instruction (Tit 2:1-10). Apparently basic skills in Christian education had been taught as well (Tit 2:1,3-4,7).

Any training program for church expansion evangelists based upon the Pauline model will have to include at least doctrine, practical ministry, administration, pedagogy and character formation. Appropriate apologetics will also be essential (Tit 1:9).

It was necessary that his disciples have an apologetic designed to answer the challenges emanating from Diana's temple and the cult of emperor worship. In each culture an appropriate systematic theology must address the questions arising from the current society. Training schools must grapple with questions from the local context.

I am convinced that Paul would encourage evaluation of a curriculum primarily on the basis of its immediate and effective contribution to the church expansion mandate in a given context. For example, Paul and his co-workers never grappled with the demands of properly applying hermeneutical principles to ensure that a twenty-centuries old message was appropriately applied to a far removed culture. The Indonesia Department of Religion has formulated a standardized curriculum for all theological schools of higher education. One of the greatest challenges we have is how to work within the regulations and still be true to our Pauline model for what is genuinely important in the training of church planting evangelists.

With all the rules, regulations and reports with which a formal accredited program must contend, it is tempting to switch to a totally informal training program. That would mean the surrender of all visas for foreign Christian workers, and would mean a total denial of the cultural need for external accreditation. Among the real advantages that Paul enjoyed were free visa movement throughout the Roman empire, and absence of governmental regulations concerning whom and how he could train.

Only with your wisdom, Lord, can we apply the vitally important lessons we have learned from the Tyrannus model within the constraints of the regulations that are on the book. But we are determined to keep trying.

13

ON TO NEW FRONTIERS

by Doug Lucas

After all this had happened, Paul decided to go to Jerusalem, passing through Macedonia and Achaia. "After I have been there," he said, "I must visit Rome also" (Acts 19:21).

All of us have known risk-takers, but perhaps the Apostle Paul, more than any other New Testament figure, was a specialist at starting things--launching out, stepping out in new ventures that others would have thought impossible. His eyes were always staring at some far off horizon where Christ's name was heretofore unknown.

Paul's travels kept him so busy that it took an accurate historian to carefully record some of his life's major accomplishments. Luke even records how Paul got his start. In Acts 11 we find Barnabas facing new challenges and opportunities in Antioch. As soon as he realizes how wide the door there has swung open, he goes and gets Saul from Tarsus (Acts 11:25). For an entire year Barnabas mentors Saul and is probably pleasantly surprised at how rapidly he progresses in theological and practical matters. The account records that the two taught "great numbers of people" and that the name "Christian" was apparently coined there to describe these new disciples. Saul, who was later to become known more widely by the Greek form of his name, Paul, has gotten his first start at evangelism.

In the years that followed we know that Paul proclaimed Christ and helped begin new works, not only in Antioch, but in the following locations:

Salamis
Paphos
Pisidian Antioch
Iconium
Lystra
Derbe
Philippi
Thessalonica
Berea
Athens
Corinth
Ephesus
Macedonia
Greece
Miletus
Jerusalem
Caesarea
Malta
Rome

In no less than twenty cities or regions, Paul initiated new beachheads for Christ's rapidly expanding kingdom. What was the secret of his success? What were the driving principles that allowed him to not only be so effective, but also to go on tirelessly in spite of the persecution and obstacles that littered his path? How did he manage to keep going, even when there were skeptics, negative responses and little support for his efforts? What enabled his works to flourish and multiply? Are there lasting foundational beacons that can and should still be guiding our efforts today? Can we share any of the same underpinnings to help us be like Paul? If so, what are some modern examples of Acts of the Holy Spirit in today's world? Is the church really alive worldwide just as it was in the days of Paul? We can find the answers to these and other questions by peering into the pages of the book of Acts.

Boldness and Determination

Let us not fool ourselves into thinking that outreach in 40 A.D. was any easier than it is today. Michael Green writes, "At whatever level in society it was attempted, evangelism in the early church was a very daunting undertaking. It was a task involving social odium, political danger, the charge of treachery to the gods and the state, the insulation of horrible crimes and calculated opposition from a combination of sources more powerful, perhaps, than at any time since" (1970:47).

Against all odds Peter, Paul, Barnabas and many others led out in an undertaking to strike a tuning fork to which much of the world would harmonize. The song they sang turned the world "right-side-up" for Christ--but it was an uphill battle. These New Testament heroes faced challenges galore--hardships, beatings, imprisonment, hunger, danger, shipwreck, cold and daily pressure (2 Co 6:4-10;11:25-28).

So how did Paul and his colleagues manage to go on? How could any mere mortal be expected to undergo so many challenges yet not only survive, but *thrive*? Perhaps the answer is to be found in Acts 4. Peter and John are imprisoned because of their unending thirst to proclaim the good news. Prior to their release, the Sanhedrin orders them not to "speak or teach at all in the name of Jesus" (4:18). They made additional "further threats" to keep them silent. However, upon their release Peter and John went directly to a prayer meeting and pleaded with God, "Now, Lord, consider their threats and enable your servants to speak your word with great boldness" (4:29). They asked God for boldness, and he answered. Only a few verses later Luke writes, "Nevertheless, more and more men and women believed in the Lord and were added to their number" (5:14).

Yes, proclamation is hard work wherever we do it, but especially cross-culturally. And often, it is not only from among non-believers that we are criticized but also from Christians as well. Paul was successful, at least in part, because he refused to give up. Down through the years others have taken up the cloak of boldness and determination and worn it effectively. William Carey, called by some the "Father of Modern Missions," is known to have had more than his share of difficulty. He buried two wives as well as little children while trying to endure the harsh climate of Central Asia. In addition, he and his cohorts underwent intense opposition even from their own countrymen. Carey's response? "I can plod," he said. "I can persevere in any definite pursuit. To this I owe everything" (Drewery 1979:25).

God is still alive and at work within our lives in the furtherance of the gospel. Obviously none of us would ever presume to have the boldness and determination of the Apostle Paul or William

Carey. But in a very personal way, God has certainly communicated his witness to members of our mission on more than one occasion, especially in the tough times.

Back in 1990, when the USSR was still the USSR, one of my friends began telling me that our mission should try to place a team in the Soviet Union. Little by little, as he repeatedly dared us to consider this, we began to wonder if he was right. One day, we received word of a special conference that was to occur in Moscow to examine the nature of outreach in Russia and neighboring republics. We called to obtain information, only to learn that it was sealed off, having been designated mainly for the Soviets themselves. Only a few Westerners would be invited. The 1100 Soviet attendees would be picked from leading churches and missions all across the country. We prayed diligently about the conference and thought it might be a landmark in helping us understand what, if any, should be our involvement there.

Out of all the organizations that had historically been working in Russia and the Eastern Block, many of whom were themselves trying to get invitations, only one-hundred individuals would be chosen, and most of these would be presenters and workshop leaders, familiar with the Russian situation.

But we felt what we suppose was some of the same boldness that was ever-present in Paul, as we began making telephone calls and sending faxes to one person after another, asking for help. As the deadline grew close for the selection of participants, our hopes seemed doomed. The head of participant selection had informed us that our mission just did not have enough experience (actually we had none) with the Soviet situation to offer anything. We begged to be able to send even a "runner" or an errand boy. We asked to deliver photocopies. We even offered to sweep the floor! We were willing to do anything to get a chance to learn more about how our mission should be involved. But it was to no avail. Nothing seemed to persuade them to give us a second thought.

That night, we read the story of the widow and the unjust judge and how she simply would not leave the judge alone until he considered her cause (Lk 18:1-8). We immediately faxed the Coordinator of the entire conference, referred to Luke 18 and explained our dilemma. We begged for reconsideration and presented ourselves as the widow in the story. An hour later, he called to say that he was so taken back by our reference to scripture that he was reconsidering and would himself issue the invitation to the conference. Obviously, we were ecstatic.

At the conference in Moscow later that year, our mission received an unlimited supply of resources and opportunities to network with mission agencies, American churches, Soviet churches and unreached people group researchers. God clearly answered our prayers. History has shown the appropriateness of that boldness, as hundreds of former atheists and agnostics have come to know Christ in southern Ukraine. Many of those have come to Christ through the efforts of others who are working with us in the region, a direct result of the networking posture that we saw modeled at the Moscow Congress. The initial base and our very foundation for the work in Ukraine began because of contacts made there. It has shaped our strategy, our target area and our long-term goals far more than any other single event. But that opportunity did not happen because of anything we had done to deserve it--the truth was, we did not deserve it. It only came about through boldness and determination. May God grant us more of it!

Effective Strategy

Paul thought out his steps in advance, long before he actually finished the sub-steps that would carry him to the next immediate stopover. We see this not only in his plan to go through Macedonia and Achaia and then on to Rome, but also when he writes, "But now there is no more place for me to work in these regions, ... I will go to Spain and visit you on the way" (Rom 15:23,28). He sought to maximize every single step.

Paul seems to have had a kind of uncanny ability to figure out an effective strategy. Green observes that Paul had a four-pronged vision that was at once *personal, urban, provincial* and *global* (1970:261). In his house in Rome, Paul invited leaders of the Jews for discussions on Christianity and the scriptures (Acts 28:23). He told Timothy, "And the things you have heard me say in the presence of many witnesses entrust to reliable men who will also be qualified to teach others" (2 Ti 2:2). Apparently, the *personal* prong was designed to create a network that would continue to expand onward and forward without hindrance.

His emphasis on *urban* outreach was just as significant. He targeted centers of learning and commerce. Antioch was the third largest city in the Roman Empire while Philippi was the Roman *colonia*. Thessalonica was the principal metropolis of Macedonia and

Corinth was then capital of Greece. Paphos was the center for Roman rule in Cyprus and Ephesus was the principal city in Asia. The urban strategy is clear, and it worked.

These cities were not chosen by sheer coincidence. Green has pointed out that Paul "seems to have made a point of setting up two or three centres of the faith in a *province*, and then passing on, and allowing the native enthusiasm and initiative of the converts to lead them to others whom they could win for Christ" (1970:263). Paul obviously had a vision for the "big picture."

In fact, his vision was so grand that he could not sit still. He moved relentlessly throughout the Mediterranean, from East to West. He had to see Rome and he even wanted to go to Spain. "It has always been my ambition to preach the gospel where Christ was not known, so that I would not be building on someone else's foundation" (Rom 15:20). Paul's parish was the world. He was a *global* thinker.

Following Paul's Lead Today

In the intervening years, it would appear that there have been precious few who have possessed Paul's unique, Spirit-led ability to size up a situation by its possibilities and its potential. But some names do come to mind. In the area of Bible translation, one immediately thinks of William ("Uncle Cam") Cameron Townsend. Billy Graham called him "the greatest missionary of our time," and Ralph Winter ranked him with William Carey and Hudson Taylor as one of the three most outstanding missionaries of the last two centuries (Tucker 1983:351). Due in large part to his early strategic leadership and steadfast commitment to the strategy God had given him, the Wycliffe Bible Translators mission agency has grown to include thousands of Bible translators and support personnel. Like Paul, he had a clear vision and a firm commitment to carry through with it.

Ministering in Ukraine

Over the past few years we have come to appreciate more and more the importance of an effective strategy, especially when coupled with some of the same type of vision and commitment that Paul had. In 1991 in Ukraine, we sensed an overwhelming mood of interest in anything and everything Western--more specifically, American.

Throughout the former Soviet Union the level of receptivity for spiritual things was at an all time high. It seemed that everyone wanted to know more about Christ.

But meanwhile the existing church had an identity problem. It had been labeled by some layers of society as being narrow, prejudiced against outsiders, eccentric and "behind the times." Furthermore, many church leaders had learned to almost play the part. They felt persecuted because they had been persecuted for some 70 years. Some behaved as if they were against outside influences.

But we were not convinced. We began to theorize that for God's kingdom to really mushroom there, all kinds of people needed exposure. That exposure needed to leave them with a favorable impression. They needed a valid opportunity and Christians needed a valid forum for witness.

In trying to formulate a strategy that would recognize these issues, we determined to hold a series of city-wide meetings that would bring in Americans from all walks of life to dialogue with the multiple layers of social strata there. We hypothesized that the middle-class and upper middle-class would be very interested in talking with foreigners and would respect their values greatly. It might sound presumptuous, but we reckoned that it would not matter what the Americans believed and presented, the Ukrainians would be interested and listen.

Part of this strategy's success was due to the fact that we were stepping into a very special window in time. We were literally the first Americans in these cities at a time when Ukrainians were trying to find out who they were going to become. They were honored to welcome successful American businessmen, farmers, doctors, nurses, teachers and religious workers. They came by the hundreds to hear presentations and to talk to their visitors. In one theater we ran a series of lectures entitled, "Mankind in Search of Meaning." Next door at an adjoining theater we had science teachers presenting a Science Film Festival. A few blocks away a group of English teachers did classwork with future Ukrainian school workers, and down the road agriculturalists held meetings in the Agriculture Institute. American doctors were in hospitals and clinics, and American collegians attracted scores of young professionals and future Ukrainian leaders.

We referred to the meetings as the Ukrainian-American Friendship Festival. But they were more than that. They were lives touching, hearts mending and minds melding. The outward events were merely symbolic for the inward openness to new values, new belief systems, new worldviews, and a new era for this people.

We have now repeated that same strategy in several other cities throughout Ukraine resulting in additional growth for the Kingdom. Obviously, the receptivity level will change over time, but the principle is the same. Find a way of fanning the natural interests that are there, present the love of Christ and the power of His message, and God brings victory.

God was the one who worked out those arrangements at the first festival. We were very green. Many mistakes were made. But in spite of ourselves, God brought hundreds of people into contact with His Word. Scores were interested in follow-up Bible studies. We were in no way prepared for the response. In the weeks that followed the festival, a series of three mailings were sent out to every person who had signaled an interest in studying about Jesus--some six-hundred people. They were invited to a theater on a Sunday evening and nearly one-hundred showed up. With the most interested core, we watched God form the nucleus of a new congregation, which in turn has, through His grace, grown to include some five-hundred active members today.

An American congregation "adopted" the church, forming a strategic partnership to reach not only local Ukrainians, but to formulate plans to reach other unreached people groups as well, especially those nearby. Following the request of the Ukrainian congregation, the American church began to focus on training leaders. God has shown that even in the midst of the most trying of times, He can triumph. All that we do is merely a trifle compared with His unending power and grace. That power and grace equips us to dream of strategies and visions that only His power could bring to reality.

Paul's Understanding of the Spiritual Vacuum

The beliefs of the early church leaders were instrumental in bringing the growth of the early church to fruition. Paul was probably the most notable, but Peter and others also felt the call of the unevangelized. Luke records Paul's words, "Now that there is no more place for me to work in these regions..." and his desire to push forward (Rom 15:23). Paul understood the concept of the spiritual vacuum. He did not disbelieve in the special status of the Jewish people--he was Jew himself. But he saw his status as a matter or role rather than position. Listen to the explanation Paul offers for his calling:

> I have written you quite boldly on some points, as if
> to remind you of them again, because of the grace
> God gave me to be a minister of Christ Jesus to the
> Gentiles with the priestly duty of proclaiming the
> gospel of God, so that the Gentiles might become an
> offering acceptable to God, sanctified by the Holy
> Spirit (Rom 15:15-16).

Paul simply had to go on to Rome. Why? Because of the spiritual vacuum there. It pulled him as a magnet pulls metal. He was drawn by an irresistible force that points to those who have not yet had a valid opportunity to receive Christ in their own culture.

Paul actually put it rather mildly, "It has always been my ambition to preach the gospel where Christ was not known" (Rom 15:20). This was apparently Paul's very reason for existence, his means of glorifying God in his life. His mandate was to go so that those "who were not told about him will see, and those who have not heard will understand" (Rom 15:21). That was the dream that drove him through all kinds of obstacles, the secret of his motivation--"those who have not heard will understand."

Others, inspired by Paul's vision and compassion for telling the untold, have sought to fill the same role. From J. Hudson Taylor's passionate plea for China to Jim Elliot's unexplainable burden for unfriendly Aucas, the spiritual vacuum is still affecting God's people today. The modern Church Growth Movement, efforts to translate the scripture for those who do not have the Bible in their own language, and the Adopt-A-People Clearinghouse all share a common affinity with that same spiritual vacuum.

Rightfully so. As one preacher asked, "Is it fair that we should hear the gospel again and again when there are those who still have not yet heard it for the first time?" Each missionary who has left home, family and friends can testify to the same driving motive that Paul expressed. With Paul it was the "Gentiles." With today's missionaries it might be Brazil or Benin, Uruguay or Ukraine, Indonesia or India. But the call is the same. Take the gospel to those who have heard it least.

A Transformed Character

Paul would not give up. The reason he worked so relentlessly was that he believed intensely in what he was teaching.   Green observes,

> These men did not spread their message because it was advisable for them to do so, nor because it was the socially responsible thing to do. They did not do it primarily for humanitarian or agathistic utilitarian reasons. They did it because of the overwhelming experience of the love of God which they had received through Jesus Christ. The discovery that the ultimate force in the universe was Love, and that this Love had stooped to the very nadir of self-abasement for human good, had an effect on those who believed it which nothing could remove (1970:236).

Paul was so struck by this timeless truth that he cried out, "The Son of God ... who loved me and gave himself for me" (Gal 2:20). He had formerly sought to annihilate those whom he would have then called wayward heretics. But he experienced a changed life and a changed heart. That change helped make him supremely effective in his ministry.

On at least two occasions, the book of Acts records Paul's testimony as having made up a significant part of his preaching (Acts 22, 26). When crowds heard him speak, they came face to face with how he once lived and saw over time the amazing transformation that God had performed on his life. In effect, Paul became an on-going living miracle because of the example of love and compassion that he lived. It was that example that helped convict the Corinthians. It was that compassion that gripped the Romans. It was that love that bonded Paul to the Ephesians.

Throughout the ages, Christ-changed lives have accounted for dozens of movies and books for all the world to know. Thousands more lives have worked behind the scenes to convict each of us of the transforming power of the gospel. We see it in the Philippian jailer (Acts 16), and even before that in the Samaritan woman that Jesus met at the well: "Many of the Samaritans from that town believed in him because of the woman's testimony" (Jn 4:39).

Today hearts and lives are still changing, and they in turn are changing others. Perhaps this was never more powerfully portrayed to me than by a young wife named Ira. Her boss summoned her to serve as translator for our American agriculturalists at the local farming institute. She was a young woman with blond hair and bright eyes that defied years of hardship in the Soviet Union.

Over the next few days as she translated, she began listening closely to the words that these believers were sharing. Within a few weeks, shortly after our agriculture team headed home to the USA, Ira gave her life to Christ. Despite my encouragement, her husband merely watched on that Sunday afternoon. Ira and I walked down into the water and she was baptized. Sasha looked on intently but gave no sign that he was ready to make the same decision. He had confessed privately to me that he was afraid. The Communists were in power. If he gave his life to Christ, it would probably mean he would lose his job.

Only a few hours passed when our phone rang. It was Sasha. He asked me to meet him in a secluded pool of the Dnepr River. That evening, in the quiet and peacefulness of a Ukrainian sunset, Sasha too made his commitment known. Sasha might as well have been baptized on the main street downtown. Within days, everyone at work knew about his decision. He began telling everyone he met about the Lord.

During her visit to the city of Kherson, Sasha's sister Tanya listened intently to her brother give his testimony. She too gave her life to Christ. Upon her return to her home in Dnepropetrovsk, Tanya, in turn, shared the gospel with her husband, also named Sasha.

Within a few short weeks we heard what we thought was bad news. Sasha of Dnepropetrovsk had become angry when he learned of Tanya's decision. But his anger was not aimed at us; it was aimed at Tanya. He was not angry because she had adopted the faith. Instead, he was angry that she had done it without him. He wanted to follow his wife's example.

Upon our arrival in Dnepropetrovsk my hopes fell. He was a difficult case. He could not bring himself to believe that Jesus really existed. If He did exist, was He really the Son of God? We spent hours discussing the Bible and Christian evidences. Three days later, Sasha too give his life to the Lord.

The Communists were still in power. But Sasha of Dnepropetrovsk did not care. Little did we know that he had been sharing the content of our discussions with yet another individual, his blood brother Slava, all weekend long. He too believed. The gospel had crossed cultures, family lines and professions. Tanya was a top research doctor. Sasha of Dnepropetrovsk was an optometrist, famous for his laser eye surgery. God's power is strong.

We did not find out until some days later just how strong He had been. Sasha and Tanya had planned on filing for divorce the very day after he had been baptized. But because of their change in heart, Sasha and Tanya are still together today, and the joy of the Lord is hard to miss in their dancing eyes. I have seen Him change hearts, transform lives and renew futures. That reality was the spark for a tremendous flame in the first century--one that still has not been extinguished. It glows brighter every day.

Teamwork

There was another reason Paul was so effective at moving on to new frontiers. He had good co-workers. Paul's greetings and closings are filled with mentionings of his colleagues and cohorts. We can observe the camaraderie that these men and women felt with one another. Paul greets Priscilla and Aquila, noting that they "risked their lives" for him (Rom 16:3-4). The entire chapter of Romans 16 is one personal commendation after another. Paul clearly worked as a team player, both in starting and in carrying out his ministry.

And why not? Barnabas had modeled it well for him. Luke tells us that Barnabas goes to Tarsus specifically to look for Saul. "And when he found him, he brought him to Antioch. So for a whole year Barnabas and Saul met with the church and taught great numbers of people. The disciples were called Christians first at Antioch" (Acts 11:26).

Antioch was Paul's training ground. At the side of Barnabas he learned the true meaning of teamwork, partnership and trust-building. So when the Holy Spirit chooses missionaries in Acts 13, it comes as no surprise that He would pick Saul and Barnabas. Traveling through the world of that day would require everything these two colleagues could muster. There would be many hardships, and they would have to depend on one another. This they did.

Even though Paul and Barnabas parted company at the beginning of the second missionary journey, Paul never forgot the lessons he had learned. He was always taking someone along with him.

"Paul and Silas", "Paul and Timothy", "Paul and Titus"--it was as if Paul operated a Bible college on foot. That is exactly what he did. The letters he sent to Timothy and Titus are nothing more than encouragement and exhortation to students from the professor of church planting.

Did Paul ever go it alone? There is at least one incident that comes to mind, and perhaps it was all Paul needed to conclude that he worked best in teams. Paul is in Athens, eagerly awaiting the arrival of his two current proteges. In what must have later looked almost like a temporary stroke of madness, Paul decided to strike out on his own toward the Areopagus. Alone and saddened by the idol-worship there, he delivers a striking message, but one that produces little fruit. He apparently is so affected by this near rejection that he leaves Athens before Silas and Timothy have a chance to arrive. Paul's efforts to start something new nearly fail. Were it not for Dionysius and Damaris, Paul might have been even more discouraged by the turn of events (Acts 17:34).

Throughout time, many have put strong emphasis on working in teams. From William Carey to Samuel Zwemer to Donald McGavran--the benefits of working together, as in the manner of Paul and Silas, have been proven again and again.

We have seen this benefit in our own mission. We now have teams working among unreached people groups scattered across the globe and we are beginning to spot a few pertinent trends. For instance, God seems to always place at least one "shepherd" on each team. You know the type--a kind of Barnabas like encourager. I am thinking of one individual in particular as I write. He has got a sixth sense for knowing when someone is hurting. In times of trouble, his compassion, mercy and tenderness are reminiscent of the 23rd Psalm. He will vouch for anyone. He almost always thinks the best of everyone's intentions. He would be willing to stand up for Saul when no one else would, or give John Mark a second chance. In short, he is the glue that can help hold the team together.

Then there is the mover and shaker, like Paul. He or she might not necessarily be gifted with intuition or people skills, but can sure get a lot of work done. Like Paul, this person would cross the world again and again if it meant one soul can be saved. He or she can profit from input from the shepherd though, especially in times of torment. In fact, some of these movers and shakers are prone to depression if they are not constantly encouraged by those with strong people skills. Paul certainly went through his down times. He depended heavily upon others to help him in those days.

There are many roles on our teams, some of which include the equipper or trainer, the creative designer, the supportive team analyst, and more. In the end, however, no two teams are alike. One thing is certain. There really is strength in numbers, especially when all those numbers are working together toward the same goal. Three strands woven together do make a cord that is not easily broken. Daily, we pray for that weaving in our own lives, even though the bending and flexing can be very taxing. We pray for boldness and determination, insight toward effective strategy, transformed characters and a new sense of teamwork. We trust God to make up the differences for our fallible human weakness. May He gain credit where there is success, and may we all work harder where there are challenges.

14

TO TURN THEM FROM THE POWER OF SATAN TO GOD

by Carolyn Butler

Then I asked, 'Who are you, Lord?' 'I am Jesus, whom you are persecuting,' the Lord replied. 'Now get up and stand on your feet. I have appeared to you to appoint you as a servant and as a witness of what you have seen of me and what I will show you. I will rescue you for your own people and from the Gentiles. I am sending you to them to open their eyes and turn them from darkness to light, and from the power of Satan to God, so that they may receive forgiveness of sins and a place among those who are sanctified by faith in me' (Acts 26:15-18).

Introduction

We sat mesmerized, Karuka and I, as we listened to Pastor Marceli and his wife tell us of their encounters with the powers of darkness. Of all the astonishing tales they told us, the most amazing was the story of a recent happening in the market place of Bukavu, on the eastern border of Zaire.

According to Marceli, a Christian woman in the market area who was having trouble selling her wares asked her neighboring vendors how they succeeded so well. They told her it was because they had *dawa*, a special charm they purchased, but they warned her that it was not for Christians.   Although she was a Christian, the woman continued to pressure them until they finally agreed to put her in contact with the power who had provided them with their secret for success.

The women went to the edge of the lake at dusk and struck the surface of the water with a stick, and waited until an unmanned canoe mysteriously appeared.   They climbed into it and went out to some distant point where the canoe with the woman in it sank to the bottom of the lake and they found themselves in the presence of the all powerful *Mwambutu*, a half-man/half-fish. He was furious when he saw they had brought a Christian with them, and held her captive while the others were sent speedily back to the surface.

The next day the husband of the woman went to the market and accosted the women, accusing them of knowing where his wife was.   When they denied it he brought a soldier who beat them until they admitted what had happened.   So the entire group--women, husband and soldier--went through the same process, going to the bottom of the lake to confront the Mwambutu. He informed them that the woman was his by rights because she, being a Christian, had willingly put herself in his power. The husband agreed to the logic of this, and they all came back to the surface, unable to challenge the evil power's right to the woman.   All charges were dropped against the women from the market.

As we walked away from Marceli's house later, our thoughts and emotions still reeling, Karuka summed it up. "As an African who has lived and studied in America, and who has a Master's degree in linguistics, one part of me wants to laugh at all of this, but the other part of me wants to dive to the bottom of the lake and snatch that woman away in the name of Jesus." I knew what she meant.

Whether or not this kind of information is credulous to us as missionaries, most Africans have witnessed or have undeniable proof that such things happen. They talk of them openly and willingly. Their worldview readily accommodates itself to the reality of the transcendent and supra-natural. They know that witch doctors and sorcerers can turn themselves into leopards or crocodiles. They know that others can call crocodiles, leopards or snakes to do their bidding. They have seen a neighbor woman's dead daughter return at night carrying huge loads of supplies for her mother, passing through locked doors and gates, a nightly drudge to her mother who paid to have her brought back to this zombie life as a slave.

I do not hesitate to claim that 98% of the Zairian population lives with the assumption that sorcerers with access to such metaphysical power exist. Many live in a daily struggle of renunciation of these traditional animistic powers. Some few actively seek to serve as channels for it. The rest of the population fits into a middle category where compromise, ambivalence and an anxious tension pulls them first one way and then another. Among them many have sought to utilize such power themselves, and almost all believe that such power has been or can be used against them and therefore regularly use some sort of charm for personal protection against metaphysical powers.

But while these kinds of happenings are foreign to our own secular culture, this is the exact kind of setting into which the Apostle Paul was sent. In his own account of his calling and commission, Paul tells us that Jesus said to him, "I am sending you to them to open their eyes and turn them from darkness to light, and from the power of Satan to God, so that they may receive forgiveness of sins and a place among those who are sanctified by faith in me" (Acts 26:17-18). Thus Paul launched himself into a battle against the devil's schemes and told his new converts in Ephesus that their struggle is "not against flesh and blood, but against the rulers, against the authorities, against the powers of this dark world and against the spiritual forces of evil in the heavenly realms" (Eph 6:12).

Satan? Rulers and powers and authorities of the dark world? Spiritual forces of evil in heavenly realms? Nothing in our secularized Western worldview, or even in our religious formation, has prepared us to deal with such possibilities. As Western missionaries we are usually abysmally unprepared to accept, let alone confront such issues.

For most of the last twenty-five years we have lived in Zaire we have been blissfully and deliberately ignorant of the belief system that governs every action and reaction of most of the Africans with whom we live and minister. African Christians, aware of this lack of insight on our part, willingly complied with our unspoken but evident reluctance to know or understand their belief system--what we call animism.

A Working Definition of Animism

The suave and well-educated young Kenyan thoughtfully pushed his cookie crumbs around on his plate as he considered my question, "Why isn't Christianity working in Africa?" He paused, "Well, I think it is because it simply does not answer the daily questions. There is too much emphasis on the life after death, and not enough solutions to the daily issues of sickness, death, fear. Christianity just has not met the survival level needs."

The issue we were discussing was the contrast between Christianity and animism. As I began studying animism I was shocked to find that not only is a large part of the world animistic by choice as well as heritage, but it is what many are turning to today. Most of the supposedly new belief systems sweeping the United States are one form or another of animism. The New Age movement is simply animism in a new guise.

The animist's worldview is spiritual rather than material. Both reality and destiny are controlled by spiritual forces. Animism is a human being's attempt to control the present and determine his or her own destiny by the manipulation of spiritual forces. This manipulation requires the knowledge and use of rituals, charms, spells, rites and sacrifices which are determined and prescribed by a person who serves as an intermediary, a channel, a medium between the petitioner and the metaphysical power source.

Clinton Arnold has written about this manipulation. He uses the term "magic" to define the way the spirit world is used.

> The overriding characteristic of the practice of magic throughout the world is the cognizance of a spirit world exercising influence over virtually every aspect of life. The goal of the magician is to discern the helpful spirits from the harmful ones and learn the distinct operations and the relative strengths and authority of the spirits. Through this knowledge, means can be constructed for the manipulation of the spirits in the interest of the individual person. With the proper formula, a spirit-induced sickness can be cured, a game won, sexual passions enhanced, etc. Conversely, great harm can be brought to another person through the utterance of a curse (Arnold 1992:18).

Ritualistic rites are performed at birth and death, and virtually every other significant event in between--sickness, marriage, planting, harvesting, traveling, buying and selling. Charms are tied on a baby's body at birth, adapted and changed throughout life, and passed on to the next generation at death. There are charms and potions to prevent sickness for a child, danger for a traveler, loss of a spouse's love. Even athletes have charms, and teams have their own witch doctors. Government and political leaders have their private sorcerers and witch doctors on salary.

The charms, spells and fetishes for manipulating the spirit world are obtained through people variously known as witch doctors, sorcerers, diviners, and medicine men--what Arnold termed as magicians. To illustrate the scope and variety of terms, I list the Swahili names that differentiate between these channels of power. While there is wide disagreement among our Zairian friends as to which name applies to which office, all agree that these categories exist. A *mulozi* is one who employs curses and has the power to do either evil or good; a *mufumu* has some elementary spiritual power but operates mostly by deceiving and manipulating clients through psychology and fear; a *muchawi* has real magical powers that are sold for a high price, always for evil purposes. A *muganga* is one who uses native cures and potions, herbs, leaves and roots, and charges only for the medicine, with or without accompanying spell or ritual. This latter category is what almost all sorcerers claim to be and do, but in fact very few of them qualify for this more positive sounding variety.

Two issues must be clarified. There is a legitimate concern about our possible opposition to what is recognized as natural medicines used by medicine men or women. It is true that Zairians know how to use the bark of the quinine tree as an anti-malarial and the leaves of the eucalyptus tree as a decongestant. Countless other herbs, roots and leaves prove effective and inexpensive. But the only people who would use such medicines in a totally scientific way are people who have had European education where they learned the physical properties of the treatments that meet physical needs. The thousands of others administer these medicines accompanied by some murmured incantation and symbolic gesture, putting their faith more in the rite than in the medicine.

An African pastor illustrated this point clearly in his own teaching on the subject. He said: If I am walking down the path with a member of my church and I say that I have a headache, many times the person accompanying me will say: "Oh, pastor, I know something that will help you." As we walk along my friend scans the bushes and leaves carefully and finally finds the right plant, and plucks off a few leaves. If he hands the leaves directly to me and says, "Here, take these leaves and chew them," I chew them and probably my headache will go away. But if he plucks the leaves and turns his back to me, blowing and muttering over the leaves before he gives them to me, I will not take it. Because then he is not asking me to use the leaves, he is asking me to use sorcery.

Secondly, there is also a legitimate concern for African traditions and culture. The practices I am referring to in this article in a negative sense are the acts of sorcery used as animistic rituals. My intention is not to denigrate or criticize the rich traditions of Zairian culture. On the contrary, the concepts of the extended family, veneration for the aged, adoration of children, respect for the ancestors and many others are exemplary. I value the lessons I have learned from African culture as some of the most beneficial gifts in my life. My spiritual worldview, formed by African Christians, is something I cherish and attempt to pass on to my children.

Because of the variety of terms used thus far and for the sake of clarity, I define sorcery as the use of power gained from the assistance or control of evil spirits. A sorcerer, then, is one who uses such spiritual power. Any reference to traditions, habits or customs in the negative sense in this article refer to some use of sorcery.

The Missionary Role as Servant and Witness

Missionaries have a role in turning people from the power of Satan to the power of God. We shall now examine certain principles that relate to that role as we attempt to work with God in moving people out of animism.

We Must View the Gospel as Light

It is significant that Jesus said to Paul that he would send him to be a "witness of what you have seen of me and what I will show you" (Acts 26:16). Before we missionaries go to be servants and witnesses in another culture, we must experience for ourselves the reality of Jesus' claim to be the light, the truth and the way. If we go on mere classroom information about the gospel, whatever our motivation, we will almost immediately find ourselves confronted with the inadequacy of our faith in what we are offering. To offer Christ to a person of another culture and religious belief without having personally experienced the truth of Jesus is to court disaster.

Our association with peoples of other cultures and religious beliefs must evidence respect and love for them. Many people of other religions practice their beliefs with a devotion and sincerity that leaves us ashamed of our half-hearted mediocrity and may cause us to doubt the value of the gospel. Our own lack of faith in the gospel can negate its value for us. What possible benefit can Christianity offer devout Muslims or Hindus or whatever group we associate closely with?

The truth is that the gospel is good news. The death of Christ on the cross breaks the power of sin and conquers Satan. Through Christ's death we have access to God, we have freedom from sin, we have power over Satan and all his demons. The Bible says that there is no other name under heaven and earth through which people will be saved (Acts 4:12). This is not an odious and judgmental message to other cultures; neither is it wrong to offer this truth.

The mistake is not that we offer Christianity to another culture--it is that we offer it so poorly. If the gospel, stripped of its American trappings, could be offered in its simplicity and practicality it would be seen as good news because it deals with the innate needs of every culture. That universal need is a response to the issue of sin, retribution, forgiveness from a higher power, and reconciliation between persons.

Our son was killed in September of 1993 when the UNICEF camp in northern Kenya where he served as a pilot was overrun by bandits. As a result of the attack the camp was closed. Although the government and local authorities profess to be unable to identify those responsible for the attack, it is obvious that the local people know who did it and why. The rumor persists that the three local clans of the area have gotten together and offered restitution in the form of 100 camels to help appease their collective guilt over what happened. We easily picture wise old men, the tribal sages, consulting long hours in their council huts resorting to their ancient tribal laws and their Muslim traditions and coming up with this amount of payment--amounting to over $25,000.

Consider the impact if someone could go to them right now and say, "You do not need to do this. Your forgiveness is not contingent upon restitution. God/*Allah*/*Mungu* has already paid it for you." Now that is good news! Sociologically, religiously, emotionally, financially, psychologically--that's good news.

Unfortunately, few of us have experienced that total adequacy of the gospel in the way Paul did. Thus we are unqualified to be the kind of witness he was. If missionaries are to minister effectively in an animistic culture, not only must we witness the adequacy of the gospel, we must also recognize the inadequacy of our own religious worldview.

We Need to Recognize the Reality of the Spiritual World

Jesus told Paul that he was sending him to the Gentiles to "open their eyes" (Acts 26:18). I suspect if He were commissioning us directly today, Jesus would most likely counsel us to open our eyes. Until we are able to discern the spiritual world, we are totally unable to open the eyes of our listeners to turn them from darkness to light. Until we ourselves see and understand the darkness, we have no light to offer.

Our scientific worldview has conditioned us to believe, or to profess to believe, only what we can see and measure. This has accounted for the justifiable criticism that what missionaries in Africa have done most successfully is secularize the people they work with. Many missionaries who have spent enough time on the mission field to know the language and culture well find themselves still virtually incapable of power encounter because of an inadequate and biased religious formation. Those of us who were taught in the classroom that the age of miracles closed with the finalizing of the Canon are not equipped to see the invisible, expect the impossible or deal with the metaphysical.

When Marceli and his wife recount their battles with spiritual forces and how they had sat up all night praying and fasting with their children and Christian neighbors while sorcerers encircled their house and supra-natural forces beat on the walls and roof, they also close with joyous laughter and clapping, spontaneous praise for how the Holy Spirit delivered them. Every time I listen to this man who deals regularly with both evil spirits and the Holy Spirit, I realize with something of a shock that I do not really believe in either.

We Dare Not Underestimate the Power of Evil

Jesus told Paul that He was sending him to "turn them from darkness to light, and from the power of Satan to God" (Acts 26:18).

There is no attempt in the New Testament writings to ignore, discount or minimize the power of Satan, or the fact that there is a dark world that has its own rulers and authorities and powers. There are forces of evil in the heavenly realms. This is the darkness that we are to turn people from. It is the power of Satan, and we must understand it for what Jesus and Paul knew it to be.

Because we do not actively believe in Satan, we underestimate the power of genuine sorcerers. The sheer determination, years of strict discipline and education, fierce asceticism and centuries of accumulated knowledge of evil make them formidable enemies. Their willingness to be used by Satan as his instruments for evil in this world makes them active enemies. Sorcerers in an area just south of our home claim to have killed a missionary because she threatened to denounce in church some of their ritualistic practices. Her sudden death by what we assumed was a heart attack is seen by all the African Christians I know as death caused by a curse.

Missionaries are often skeptical of the actual amount of power any sorcerer can legitimately claim. It is true that much of sorcery is psychological, playing on superstitions and gullibility of primitive people. When people are ready and primed to see something or hear something, they certainly are capable of seeing, hearing and feeling things that really do not exist. Shrewd observers of their own people, clever at interpreting gestures and habits, these feared and respected charlatans can manipulate themselves into places of great power. Converted witch doctors are the first to admit, often with great hilarity, the tricks they have played on unsuspecting people. But these new converts become abruptly cold and serious when questioned about Satanic power.

Many are also masters at building their power in reverse, that is to say claiming to have done something after the fact. By arguing backward from certain events, they are able to add to their own power by claiming to have caused them. My husband and I have made spiritual warfare our priority in Zaire during the last three years, and hopefully disrupted some community patterns. This has consequently riled many practitioners of sorcery and probably deprived them of some trade. There is no doubt in my mind that many have claimed responsibility for the recent death of our son. Only time will tell how God uses that incident and our reaction to it to turn it into a victory.

Two comments need to be made here. People's belief in and reliance on such power is not contingent on whether the power is real or imagined. It is equally sinful to seek another power source whether that force is fraudulent or demonic. The willingness, the desire to rely on any other power source than God is what is forbidden.

The other comment is that such power does exist, coming from other power sources than God. Scriptures never assume there are no other gods. The hundreds of scriptural admonitions against idolatry and following false gods rather assume that other power sources exist. The magicians in Pharaoh's court matched Moses and Aaron's signs through the first four miracles, and then acknowledged that the hand of God had defeated them. The witch of Endor did in fact raise Samuel from his grave to converse with Saul. The prophesies in the New Testament point to an increase of this power in the last days. The issue lies more in asking why such evil cosmic and metaphysical power would not be available in this day and age rather than asking how it could.

Although the entire Bible is saturated and punctuated regularly with information about the spiritual world, until we are actually searching for it, Satan blinds our eyes to the wealth of information accessible to us. One of the most enlightening studies I have embarked upon in the past couple of years has been to make use of my computer concordance to search out spiritual warfare vocabulary.

I well remember the day I fed the words "sorcery, sorcerer, magic, magician, spells, divination, charms, witch, witchcraft, and gods" into my computer word search, pressed the command to print them out, and went into the kitchen to get a cup of coffee. While there I got delayed with lunch preparations and realized some 10 minutes later that the printer was still printing. Alarmed, I ran into the office to find it on page 16 of what turned out to be 20 pages of text. One of the things we must do is open our minds to the truth of scripture and allow ourselves to be equipped with the truth God has given us for dealing with metaphysical powers in spiritual warfare.

As long as missionaries treat animistic beliefs as superstition, our response will be to use our Western mentality and education to correct a faulty and deficient belief system. It is only if we accept the fact that--Yes, Satan has the power to turn a willing subject into an object to be used for perpetuating evil--that we will see animistic beliefs as a spiritual problem. Only then can we respond with spiritual answers.

It is essential for our own faith and for the effectiveness of our mission to others that we missionaries develop a personal theology of the supra-natural. We must pray for wisdom to read and understand the Scriptures so that we can overcome barriers of our traditions and unlearn our misinformation. Our goal is understanding the Enemy and the miraculous power we have at our disposal for defeating him. The battle to establish the Kingdom of God on earth is as much a truth encounter as a power encounter. Knowing the truth is our first responsibility.

Many of us who grew up believing that we possessed *The Truth* are having to rephrase that statement to say that while what we were taught and what we believed was *true*, it is not *The Truth*. God is Truth. And being Truth, He has a lot more of Himself to reveal to us than we know. My deepening understanding of spiritual powers and power encounter has been the most valuable spiritual lesson I have ever learned, and my gratitude to the African Christians who have helped me learn it is an eternal one.

Consciously Cleansing Our Lives of Satan's Strongholds

Those who live in countries where the political system is overtly corrupt must fight a constant battle to refuse to give Satan a foothold. It is essential for each missionary to work out a practical, ethical, morally accountable system for survival where legality as we know it does not exist. In spiritual terms, this means living and acting in such a way that Satan has nothing to accuse us of.

Satan can establish a stronghold in our personal lives. Missionaries do not flee personal temptations by going to the mission field. On the contrary, the pressures and tensions of another culture, the loneliness and frequent discouragement will be fertile ground for Satan to plant and nourish the same temptations and sins that flourished back home.

We Should Study the Culture and the Belief System

Understanding can best be gained by manifesting a sincere desire to comprehend and by listening with a non-judgmental attitude to a people's revelations about themselves. A sympathetic willingness to identify with the daily pressures, fears and tensions will provide a wealth of information.

Biblical passages can be good openers for gaining cultural information. Passages, such as Deuteronomy 18:9-13 will almost certainly need more detailed and specific explanation than literal translations offer. A missionary co-worker and I have spent hours sitting with African women around an open fire explaining as best we can what Swahili words for divination, interpreting omens, casting spells, being a medium and raising the dead mean. Their amazed recognition of what we are talking about has given us the names for these practices in the tribal languages of Mashi, Kilega and Kibali. Using these tribal words in our seminars and class sessions makes the Scriptural admonitions against such things come to life for the listeners.

One way to acquire such information is to ask someone in a group to recount the most interesting story she has ever heard about sorcery. This will inevitably lead to a "can you top this one" exchange, and in this non-threatening atmosphere we can pick up vocabulary and ask for explanations and clarifications. Another technique is to begin recounting something that we heard about another tribe, or something we have read about another country. This invariably leads to confidences about the people's own practices. Information gleaned in a positive setting provides the background for offering the good news of the gospel in a needed context-- light for their particular darkness.

A faithful national pastor of many years remarked with some bitterness that missionaries have spent their years in Zaire talking about love and giving and certain doctrinal distinctives, but not one of them has told how to overcome evil spirits that hold the country in captivity.

If we are not personal witnesses to and examples of a spiritual power greater than the one African Christians have evidenced in animism, there is little hope of ever making Christianity credible. Either the same power available to Moses and Elijah and Peter and Paul is available to us today, or it is not. If it is not, then all we have to offer Zairians is one more religion among many, and an inadequate one at that.

Showing the Way to a Place Among the Sanctified

When Jesus sent Paul to turn his converts from darkness to light, the goal was to be two-fold: that they may receive forgiveness of their sins, and that they may achieve a place among those who are sanctified by faith in him (Acts 26:18). We share the same goal. But how are we to best offer such guidance?

Deal with the Heart Needs

Due to our lack of expectation or even acceptance of a ready recourse to spiritual power, we have not dealt with the genuine spiritual needs of the people to whom we have gone to minister.

Because our contribution as missionaries has not dealt with their genuine needs--the heart and spirit needs--the Zairian Christians have been forced to continue with or turn back to their traditional power sources. For physical, technical and financial help they come to us. For spiritual, emotional and heart needs they turn/return to sorcery.

Life is a matter of survival in Zaire where two out of five children die, where an entire family is wiped out by cholera. It is the centuries old rites and rituals that provide means for coping, that provide a reason for, an explanation of, and perchance a rescue from such disasters. Missionaries must find ways to make the gospel minister to and respond to these needs. One of the ways to do this is to build on the almost certain belief in one transcendent God.

Emphasize the Character of God

It is almost unanimously accepted among all the peoples of Africa that there is a supreme God, a good God, who created the world and who once lived in close fellowship with people, but has now withdrawn. To contradict this, we prepared studies of the evidences of the close and constant supervision this Holy God still maintains. In this survival society we emphasize the regularity of the growing seasons, the unvarying life cycle of conception and birth, the reproduction of plants and animals after their own kind. We translated the traditional characteristics of omnipotence, omniscience, and omnipresence into a song put to a familiar tune so that the illiterate also can learn and remember. At every seminar we teach this song.

The most effective passages of Scripture will vary of course with the culture. Because of the typically African belief in a departed deity, one of the most effective passages we use is from John, where Jesus says, "My Father is always at his work to this very day, and I, too, am working" (Jn 5:17). Since Zairian culture is so closely tuned to nature and seasons, we emphasize that every seed planted grows because God is working. Every time a man and woman conceive a child, it is because God is working. The promise of James is also well received: "Every good and perfect gift is from above, coming down from the Father of the heavenly lights, who does not change like shifting shadows" (Jas 1:17).

Most of all we insist that God is love, and that everything God does for his people is motivated by love, even though it may appear to be hard for the moment. Satan is evil and is motivated by hate, and everything that he does is for our harm, although it may appear good for the moment.

Build on the Idea of Blessing and Cursing

The passage in Deuteronomy 18:9-13 lists the things that are an abomination to God, things for which his curses will be poured out, not only on the one practicing them but upon their children and grandchildren, a powerful incentive in Zaire where family is all-important. When we read down through that list of strange Swahili words it evokes no response. But when we begin to explain what sacrificing children, using divination and interpreting omens means in their own tribal language, giving examples of the intestines of animals studied and human body parts being used as medicine, it inevitably evokes strong reaction because all these evils are actively practiced. Then we carefully study the passages about blessing, what kind of lives God's people must actively live to receive blessing, not only upon their own lives but the lives of their children, grandchildren, great-grandchildren to the seventh generation.

We as Western Christians do not understand this concept of blessing and cursing either, which probably explains why we have not passed it on. How much of the good in our lives is the result of God's blessing because of our parents and grandparents and past generations of faithful leaders and people who made an attempt to honor and follow the rules and precepts of God? How much of the evil we all recognize and decry now in our society is a curse of God on deliberate rejection of his laws and precepts? How much responsibility do we have as parents, responsible adults, teachers to pass this on to our own children?

Renouncing, Repenting and Reaffirming

In the early years of our mission in Zaire people were required to renounce Satan at the same time they confessed Christ as part of their salvation process. The custom disappeared somewhere along the line and most church leaders admit that we are feeling the sad effects of that.

In an attempt to remedy the situation, we have compiled a statement of affirmation and renunciation which we now explain in two-day seminars for church leaders, asking them to study with us, pray at home overnight and then make a public commitment re-affirming their faith in Christ. After a prayer of repentance, they renounce any foothold Satan may have in their lives because of sins, either their own or their parents, renounce the power of any curse that has been put on them or that they caused to be put on another. In addition they promise to burn or destroy all charms, fetishes, and idols in their possession. Typically, about half of the people attending will make the commitment.

While this system has been effective, we have made some mistakes we might have avoided. We started with the women because that is where we saw evidence of the biggest need. We should have started with the men who are the recognized leaders of the church, with them and their wives. Then we should have moved into the churches, starting with the preachers and elders and deacons and their wives.

Replacing Traditional Protection with Christian Protection

Although it is seldom openly verbalized, the question most women struggle with is, "If I give up all the tangible charms, what do I get in return? If I take the bracelet that my mother gave me off my baby, what do I put there instead? If I take down the medicine given by the sorcerer from my doorway to keep the spirits out, what do I put there instead? If I do not have a feather to fasten in my hair to help me sell in the market, how will I earn money to buy food for the day?"

In our search for effective methods I had an interesting discussion with a Jesuit priest about the admitted advantage the Roman Catholics have of replacing traditional charms with medals and rosaries. His conclusion was that we cannot remove anything of value without replacing it with something more valuable. With what can we legitimately replace traditional charms? Our attempts have admittedly been of questionable success. Giving out a small New Testament to those who made the public statement to renounce the use of sorcery resulted in one wizened lady clasping the missionary's hand and exclaiming, "Now I have my ticket to heaven!" Still, I believe the idea is worth consideration and possible adaptation.

To combat the problem of animistic charms, church leaders are starting to customize their prayer for new babies in the church service, touching the child at the neck, the wrists and around the waist where charms would usually be fastened. Families who decide to take down charms and fetishes from their homes and compounds call for groups of Christians to come and stand in all those places and pray for blessing and protection. One congregation regularly has blessing services for new business ventures. We encourage blessing prayers on fields at planting and harvesting times.

In a congregation where the church leaders and their spouses make the commitment of renouncement and reaffirmation together, the next step is the formation of a group that serves as a spiritual clinic for church members. They make the decisions about which are acceptable traditional medicines and how to use them. They pray for release from any kind of demonic hold, removal of curses and overcoming temptations. These difficult spiritual decisions are made by the entire church family in the security of a Christian environment.

Our Main Ministries Must Always be the Normative Ones

One thing we have personally determined our role not to be is involvement in confrontation with sorcerers or sorcery. We have seen our role as equipping national church leaders who, given the Scriptures, are much better prepared to deal with the issues and personalities than we are. One of the most amazing things our awareness of spiritual warfare has shown us is that most of our church leaders were already dealing with this issue. In many cases they had taken great care to prevent us from knowing that, fearing either our scorn or our incredulity, or both. Now we consider ourselves working as a team. Our role is one of active participation in teaching of and intercession for those God specially gifts for this ministry.

Our priority is still given to evangelism, translation, healing, leadership training, teaching--whatever the Lord originally called us to do. To focus on Satan and his power in any way is to lose our focus on God and our calling. Few of us are going to be gifted for power encounters, and even if so, it is by the power of the Holy Spirit rather than our own power. Paul's priority of opening people's eyes so that they may turn from the darkness to light and from the dominion of Satan to God must be our priority calling also.

Conclusion

We are not overestimating our own task by claiming Jesus' commission of Paul as our very own. Rather, we are under-rating our calling and ministry if we do less. Jesus sends all of us to our particular Gentiles to open their eyes and turn them from darkness to light. No doubt when we are obedient to this calling we too shall very possibly be seized and tried, maybe even be threatened with death. But we will have God's help to the very end.

15

WAS PAUL A SHORT TERM MISSIONARY?

by A. Wayne Meece

They arranged to meet Paul on a certain day, and came in even larger numbers to the place where he was staying. From morning till evening he explained and declared to them the kingdom of God and tried to convince them about Jesus from the Law of Moses and from the Prophets. Some were convinced by what he said, but others would not believe. They disagreed among themselves and began to leave after Paul had made this final statement: "The Holy Spirit spoke the truth to your forefathers when he said through Isaiah the prophet: " 'Go to this people and say, "You will be ever hearing but never understanding; you will be ever seeing but never perceiving." For this people's heart has become calloused; they hardly hear with their ears, and they have closed their eyes. Otherwise they might see with their eyes, hear with their ears, understand with their hearts and turn, and I would heal them.' "Therefore I want you to know that God's salvation has been sent to the Gentiles, and they will listen." For two whole years Paul stayed there in his own rented house and welcomed all who came to see him. Boldly and without hindrance he preached the kingdom of God and taught about the Lord Jesus Christ (Acts 28:23-31).

When Roland Allen's book, *Missionary Methods: St. Paul's or Ours?*, first appeared in America in 1962, the material was already forty years old. The book is almost seventy years old now and the material is as timely as ever. In the introduction, Allen spoke of problems relative to mission methods of his time:

> Men have wandered over the world, 'preaching the word', laying no solid foundations, establishing nothing permanent, leaving no really instructed society behind them, and have claimed St Paul's authority for their absurdities... They have wandered from place to place without any plan or method of any kind, guided in their movements by straws and shadows, persuaded they were imitating St Paul on his journey from Antioch to Troas. Almost every intolerable abuse that has ever been known in the mission field has claimed some sentence or act of St Paul as its original (1962:5).

Allen's principles of missions are timely, but they are frequently ignored, and short term missionaries are among the guilty. Short term missions has been called the wave of the future, and though some believe they can replace career missionaries, others are not convinced. In 1970, short term workers made up only 10% of the total missionary force; today it is 40% (Paddock 1992:630). While short termers will not totally replace the career missionary, they are a major portion of the total mission force and are here to stay. Our challenge is to find a way to use them efficiently and effectively.

The question at hand is whether the life and work of Paul can serve as a model for modern short term mission work. There is a strong temptation to answer in the affirmative. Paul did not stay long in many cities, and his amazing success is a tempting lure to success-oriented people. Yet there is a danger in making hasty conclusions and seeking short-cuts to lofty goals. Balanced against Paul's short time in some places are his two and three year ministries in others. We need to take another look at Paul as a model for modern missions, particularly short termers.

What is a Short Term Missionary?

There is no generally accepted definition of a short term missionary. Many have discussed the question of short term workers, some with favor and others being quite critical. Reading the material can be confusing, and makes one wonder if all are discussing the same subject. Paddock suggested that a short termer is someone who stays on the mission field from a few days to two years. He went on to list several categories of short term missionaries: 1) college interns and summer workers--usually students who spend eight to twelve weeks under the supervision of a missionary; 2) volunteers in construction--men and women who use their vacation time to do construction projects in another culture; 3) one-year to two-year volunteers-- people who can do specialized projects; and 4) vocational Christian service--"tent-making" missionaries (1992:630).

Most Bible colleges require some form of internship before graduation and some sponsor mission internships with scholarships from mission funds raised by students and faculty. Many churches encourage their members, particularly their youth, to become involved in short term mission projects to the mutual benefit of the church and the mission field.

There is a legitimate and useful place for short term workers on most mission fields. They can be a great help and encouragement to both missionaries and local Christians. They can also be a blessing to their home churches by bringing a first-hand perspective on their mission projects. Many career missionaries made one or more short term trips before committing themselves to long term work.

Another Kind of Short Termer

Another kind of short term missionary does not fit any of the above categories. These are people who have made a career of short term mission jaunts all over the world. They saturate the churches with mass-mailed literature lauding their accomplishments. Some of these reports are questionable at best. One group published a story about a church they "started" in a French speaking West African country. With the report was a picture of the new Christians standing in front of their meeting place. The church sign was in English. Why would a church in a French speaking country have a sign in English to announce its name and times of worship?

Short term workers have been known to enter an area and ignore the missionaries living there. Claims are made as if the Gospel had never reached the area. There seems to be a deliberate policy of not working with the established church.

This second class of short term workers is in contrast to the short termers defined and described by Paddock. The first sees short term missions as an aid to the career missionary and the local church; the second sees short term missions as a career in itself. The first believes that short term workers stand beside the local church; the second believes that short term missions can stand alone and be a substitute or replacement for career missionaries.

Personal experience indicates that short term workers cannot establish churches. They may start them, but the infant churches wither without adequate discipling, and after becoming disillusioned and discouraged they soon die.

Short term missionaries went to Ivory Coast and "started" several churches, leaving a poorly trained local leader to care for the churches. The leader was promised funds for his own living, materials and equipment to do his work, and funding to build church buildings. None of these promises were fully kept, so he was forced to move into another area of the country to find employment, leaving the churches with no one to help them. Later, when time and personnel made it possible for missionaries to go into the area to work, only one or two individuals could be found and it was necessary to start all over again. A church had been started and then left alone to die. The only thing that can be said about such methods is that they are short term--they are not mission methods in any credible sense.

Paul and the Gospel Unhindered

The book of Acts closes in a most unexpected way, drawing attention to Paul's mission methodology and Luke's purpose in writing the book. Paul is in prison and the outcome of his ministry is uncertain. Luke has traced Paul's long successful mission career, yet the book closes without a word about Paul's trial. What was important in Luke's eyes, as Bruce notes, was that "the Gospel was proclaimed freely in Rome through the lips of its chief messenger" (1988:511). The Gospel was preached "without hindrance", a legal term meaning "without let"--Luke's way of saying that Christianity was a legitimate and legal religion. Paul was a Roman citizen, a prisoner who had appealed to Caesar, and who was waiting for trial under guard. Yet he freely received anyone who came and for two full years preached the Gospel of Christ without hindrance.

First for the Jew

Even in Rome where a church already existed, Paul carefully adhered to the principle he had set forth in Romans 1:16--to preach the Gospel "first for the Jew." He could not go to the synagogues, as he did without exception during his missionary journeys, but the Jews could come to him. On two occasions large numbers came and listened respectfully to his day long presentation of the message of Christ. Like most of the Jews that Paul had encountered, they were divided in their response. Most refused to believe that Jesus was the Messiah, leaving Paul no choice but to spend his efforts preaching to the Gentiles of Rome.

"First for the Jew" was a principle that Paul followed without fail though he had been commissioned by the Lord to be the Apostle to the Gentiles. Why? What plan or program of evangelism did Paul follow? What other principles guided him? Allen's classic work is again useful. He points out that Paul preached in the centers of Roman government, in the synagogues, within the Greek culture, and in cities that were centers of trade (1962:13).

The synagogues, with their Jewish communities and large numbers of proselytes and God-fearing Gentiles attached to them, gave Paul a ready audience for the Gospel message. Those who worshiped and studied in the synagogues were familiar with the Old Testament scriptures and could easily follow Paul's long and complicated reasoning concerning the promised Messiah. Converts from synagogue audiences were a well trained source of leadership who made it possible for Paul to appoint elders and deacons in the churches relatively soon after they began. They spoke the same language and shared the same culture, so there were few cultural barriers to overcome.[1]

Notable Exceptions

There are so few exceptions to Paul's preaching in synagogues first that they are worthy of note. The first was at Lystra (Acts 14:8-20). There is no mention of a synagogue, so Paul's point of contact was a miracle which drew the undivided attention of the town. The people believed Paul and Barnabas were a visitation from the gods Zeus and Hermes, so the priest of Zeus prepared a sacrifice to honor them. Since Paul and Barnabas did not understand the local language the matter was far advanced before they realized what was happening. This embarrassing and dangerous incident would never have happened if the people had been Jews or if Paul and Barnabas understood the local language. The outcome was disastrous. Paul's rejection of their overtures embarrassed the priests of Zeus and disappointed the people of the town. Visiting Jews antagonistic to the Gospel won the crowd over and Paul was stoned and left for dead. Only a notable miracle prevented the premature end of Paul's missionary career.

The text mentions disciples in Lystra, and Timothy was from the area, so the effort there was not fruitless. But Paul did not allow such an incident to happen again. He avoided trouble and confrontation whenever possible, often at great pain and anguish over the welfare of the young churches he was forced to leave. He worked with contacts who had some knowledge of God, he preached and wrote in Greek, and he expected his preaching and letters to be understood and obeyed.

Another incident is in Philippi (Acts 16:11-40). Paul was in Philippi by the Lord's direct intervention. The Spirit had prevented him from going to Asia and Bithynia, and a vision called him to Macedonia (Acts 16:6-10). Evidently there was no synagogue in Philippi, so Paul and his companions found a group of God-fearing women who met for prayer along a river outside the city. Some of these women, including Lydia, were the first converts. Lydia's home became the meeting place for the church that grew from that nucleus.

It would be interesting to know how much the experience at Lystra influenced Paul's work in Philippi. Did he suffer the exasperating taunts of the demonized girl for many days because he knew that if he healed her he would be forced to leave town or worse? Paul preferred to start with a Jewish women's prayer meeting rather than risk a totally heathen audience such as at Lystra.

After leaving Philippi when "they had passed through Amphipolis and Apollonia, they came to Thessalonica, where there was a Jewish synagogue" (Acts 17:1). The implication of Luke's reference to the synagogue is that they passed through Amphipolis and Apollonia because these cities had no synagogue. Had Paul made a mistake in Lystra? Neither he nor Luke suggest it, but it seems significant that after Lystra, Paul meticulously followed the guideline, "First for the Jew," which usually meant he began with the local synagogue.

How Long is Short Term?

Luke takes pains to indicate how long Paul stayed in one place. He counted the number of Sabbaths in Thessalonica, though it is likely Paul stayed longer than the three weeks Luke mentions (Acts 17:2). In Ephesus, Luke mentions periods of three months and two years (Acts 19:8,10). Again, it is likely that Paul stayed longer in Ephesus than the time mentioned, perhaps as long as three years, since Luke later says that he stayed in Asia "a little longer" after he had decided to make a trip to Jerusalem (Acts 19:22). Gaertner is correct when he suggests that the term 'missionary journeys' should not be understood as "established itineraries with brief stops in every case. In some instances a city like Corinth or Ephesus will become the headquarters for the missionaries' work for extended periods of time" (1993:202).

More often than not Paul's stay in a place was cut short by circumstances beyond his control. Only in Ephesus did he get to stay as long as he felt it necessary. Yet even there his ministry closed with a riot stirred up by the silver-smiths who were losing business because of his ministry. Paul was reluctant to go back to Ephesus but asked the elders to later meet him at Miletus (Acts 20:17-37).

Starting and Establishing Churches

In places where Paul was not able to stay for long periods of time he found ways to satisfy the needs of the converts he left behind. The first of these was a system of meticulous revisitation. When Paul reached the end of his first missionary journey at Derbe, instead of going on to Antioch he turned back to face his enemies. Reese observes that, "One of the most important points of Paul's missionary method comes to view at this time. Not only are men to be won to Christ, but the converts must be conserved" (1976:516).

None of Paul's missionary journeys were totally devoted to breaking new ground. In the first two, as much as half of his time was spent revisiting the churches to strengthen the disciples (Acts 14:22; 15:41; 18:23). During the third missionary journey there is no indication that Paul preached in any place where he had not been before. He spent more time and energy encouraging and establishing churches than he did in starting churches.

Involved in strengthening the disciples was the appointment of elders in each church. Many early converts were devout Jews, proselytes and God-fearing Gentiles. Some were elders in the Jewish community of faith. We must not underestimate the importance of spiritual gifts by the laying on of the hands of the Apostles. Spiritual gifts gave the churches spiritual power and divine guidance.

Teamwork

Paul developed a method of teamwork that was effective and is still useful today. When it was necessary for Paul to leave a town before the work was done, as was the case in Philippi, Thessalonica and Berea, one or more of the team were left behind. Luke stayed in Philippi for as much as five years, rejoining Paul again on his trip to Jerusalem at the end of the third missionary journey.[2] Silas and Timothy stayed at Berea while Paul went alone to Athens (Acts 17:15). Paul sent Timothy back to the Thessalonians from Athens because he could not bear not knowing how they were (I Th 3:1-2).

Working as a team, Paul and his co-workers had an influence over wide areas. Both Paul and Luke emphasize the regional or provincial scope of their ministry. Cities such as Antioch in Syria, Corinth in Macedonia, and Ephesus in Asia gave Paul and his teams a base from which to reach the entire region. He may have had the same vision for Rome when he asked them to help him on his way to Spain (Rom 15:24). Paul never abandoned the team concept. Late in his life when he was in prison he told Timothy about various team members he had dispatched to other places, lamenting, "Only Luke is with me" (2 Ti 4:9-12).

Cutting the Ties

Paul told the Ephesian elders that they would never see his face again and reminded them of their responsibility for guarding and feeding the church (Acts 20:31-32). It is likely a similar speech was repeated to the elders in every church on his last trip around the Aegean Sea headed for Jerusalem.

From Corinth he had written to Rome saying that "there is no more place for me to work in these regions," so he had already decided that he would not return (Rom 15:23). The trip covered the greater portion of a year from the time he left Ephesus and returned, and it is hard to imagine that he would have had less feeling for the elders at Corinth, Berea, Thessalonica, Philippi or Troas than he did for Ephesus. The point is simple--Paul did not start churches and leave them on their own. He stayed with them as long as possible, visited them often, sent others to help them, and finally wrote letters to most if not all of them.

Letters to Young Churches

It is not necessary to belabor the importance of Paul's letters to the churches. The fact that they make up the majority of the New Testament Scriptures and are a source of doctrine and inspiration for discipling today makes them immeasurably more important to the Scripture hungry churches that first read them. Paul and his co-workers were only the beginning of a long line of missionaries and teachers who would come and go, but the letters he wrote remain with the church as the apostles's doctrine to this day. They were the final step in strengthening and establishing the church.

Was Paul a Short Term Missionary?

Since Paul has been used as a model for short term missions, it is legitimate to ask whether Paul was a short term missionary. Did Paul do any of the things that can be legitimately called short term missions today?

Paul the Tent-maker

Paul was not short term in the sense that he gave part of his time and energy to a mission project while carrying on his profession somewhere else. From the time of his conversion he gave his life totally to spreading the Gospel. He was not an itinerant tent-maker who used his spare time for missions. It was exactly the opposite. His work as a tent-maker was a means of supporting his mission efforts. Paul refused to take support from the new churches while he was beginning a work, yet he gladly accepted help from these same churches when he moved on to another place (1 Co 4:12; 9:15).

Length of Term

The time Paul spent with each church was not necessarily short, even when the account given in the book of Acts is brief. Paul's work in Galatia--Iconium, Lystra, and Derbe--seems to fit the short term scenario, but a closer look shows otherwise. Paul personally visited those cities four times. He passed through that area twice during the first and at the beginning of the second and third missionary journeys. It also seems likely that Paul spent more time in that area than is implied by the brief accounts in Acts. Luke noted the opening of new territory and emphasized the spread of the Gospel throughout the world (Acts 1:8). So trips over old territory, some of which required months or years, were summarized in a few words or sentences. The beginning of the third missionary journey is told in two verses, yet it was a journey covering about 1,500 miles and would have required a minimum of several months (Acts 18:23; 19:1).

Paul's first contact with the Macedonian churches was cut short by opposition from the Jews, but he left others to help them and sent team members to visit them. During the third missionary journey he passed through Macedonia twice and spent considerable time there. Luke tells of Paul's trip through Macedonia from Ephesus to Corinth and back in six verses, but this trip covered the better part of a year (Acts 20:1-6). Paul's seeming short time with the Galatian or Macedonian churches cannot be used as an excuse for starting a church and then leaving it before it is able to stand on its own.

Paul's short stay in many places was seldom a matter of choice. Paul was literally run out of almost every city in which he preached, causing him great anguish concerning the welfare of the churches he had left behind. In Thessalonica he had been forced to leave because of opposition from the Jews. While Paul was waiting in Athens he sent Timothy to find out about their faith.

Paul's practice of staying a short time in some of the places he preached cannot be used as a model for short term missions. His leaving created problems that had to be solved with repeated visits by him and his team members. Left to his own devices, Paul stayed in Corinth and Ephesus from two to three years. Some of his team members stayed in one place even longer.

It was not Paul's practice to spend a week or two in a place, baptize a few people, organize a church, appoint elders and then leave them on their own. Those who do so and use Paul as their example misunderstand Paul and his methods altogether.

Paul as a Mono-Cultural Missionary

In the Roman empire there was one language and rule of law, free travel and trade, and a Jewish community and synagogue in most major cities. Paul's principle of going first to the Jew would be difficult to follow today among the unreached peoples of the world. There are bridges of God in most societies, but nothing to compare with the common ground that Paul had with the Jews. The preaching of the Gospel to the Jews was not fruitless. Paul mourned the fact that the result was so small. But the converts from the Jews and God-fearing Gentiles attached to the synagogues provided the foundation upon which the church was built. The Apostles, the early evangelists, and large numbers of early Christians were Jewish, though the ratio of Jew to Gentile grew smaller as the church spread farther from Jerusalem.

Luke's unusual and sudden close to Acts indicates the end to an era of church history. From there the church moved largely outside the realm of the religious influence of the Jews and the language and law of the Greeks and Romans, going literally to the ends of the earth. Missions today is done in this new era--the era of cross-cultural missions. All missionaries must use methods appropriate to the times as well as in keeping with sound Biblical principles.

Paul's Language

Paul is not a model for the use of language in mission practice. He spoke and wrote in Greek and expected to be understood and obeyed. In most cities and towns where Paul preached Greek was the trade language. Short termers seldom take the time to learn the trade language of the people to whom they preach and almost never learn the native tongue. One of Paul's embarrassing and dangerous moments was the result of not knowing the Lycaonian language of Lystra. Short termers are often warned about such linguistic mistakes, but seldom avoid them. The result is that they are not good communicators and often create serious problems for themselves, the local Christians and the missionaries.

Some short termers are to be especially criticized for their failure to work with established missionaries and local believers who know the culture and could help them be more effective and avoid serious mistakes.

Team Building

Paul's methods of team work are not followed by many short term mission projects. With Paul, team building was a continuous process which assumed a lifetime of service, and drop-outs such as John Mark and Demas were considered "deserters" whose commitment to the Lord and His work was questionable (Acts 13:13; 15:36-38; 2 Ti 4:9,11). Paul asked team members to remain in places when he left and sent them back to help solve problems as well as carry letters. Modern short term mission teams, which are organized for a short time and disbanded, in no way compare with Paul's method of team work. Short term teams can and often do a commendable and needed job, but they are not using the same methods as Paul.

There is no record of Paul getting involved in any kind of building projects or medical programs. He did organize relief for the church in Jerusalem, and that project may come as close as anything he did to match what short termers do today.

Conclusion

Paul was not a short term missionary as the term is used today. He was committed to his task for life--world evangelism was not a sideline with him or those he gathered around him. Most of legitimate short term mission work today pales in comparison with Paul.

Short term mission work, while it may not find a model in Paul, does not need to be denigrated because of that, nor should those who participate be discouraged. I am not opposed to short term missions. My personal experience with short term missionary workers has not been all negative. Far from it. I have, in fact, recruited and used them extensively. The majority have made a positive and important contribution. They are to this day good personal friends. Several have joined the ranks of career missionaries and serve in Africa, Asia, Europe and the United States. Others are still in training and plan to use their talents and experience to serve the Lord either at home or abroad.

Luke's notion of the Gospel being preached without hindrance should be a challenge to both the career missionary and the short termer. Paul had brought the church to the close of an era; others have followed in his wake and advanced the church beyond the world of the Jews and Rome. Those who venture into new frontiers do not have a ready-made audience, a common culture or language with which to work, and in many places a government with the tolerance of Rome.

The church today must give the greatest respect and support to the missionary who will invade another culture for Christ. Their education and preparation requires years of study and hard work. It takes much time to learn another language and then many more years to translate the Bible into that language. Bridges must be found to bring the Christian message across cultural barriers that separate one ethnic group from another.

Paul did not face these language and cultural problems, and those who try to do cross-cultural missions using him as an example deceive themselves. Paul took advantage of his Jewish roots, the widespread Greek language, and the privileges of Roman citizenship because they opened doors of opportunity for him. Those advantages do not exist among most of the unreached peoples of our day.

So multiply the short term missionaries--they will always be needed as helpers, encouragers, and a source of career missionary recruits. Not everyone can or should be a career missionary, and those who can go for a short time should be encouraged. But short term missionaries will never take the place of career missionaries or fill the need for cross-cultural missions. Finding the missionaries who will go and stay for long periods of time should be our highest priority.

Endnotes

[1]Paul spoke Greek, Aramaic and likely Hebrew. See Acts 21:37-22:2.

[2]The "we" sections, which indicate Luke's presence with the team, end in Philippi (Acts 17:1), and begin again when Paul makes the journey to Jerusalem five years later (Acts 20:6).

BIBLIOGRAPHY

Ali, Abdullah Yusuf
    1993 *The Meaning of the Holy Qur'an.* Brentwood,
        Maryland: Amana Corporation.

Allen, Roland
    1962 *Missionary Methods: St. Paul's or Ours?*
        Grand Rapids: William B. Eerdman's Pub. Co.

Arnold, Clinton
    1992 *Ephesians: Power and Magic.* Grand Rapids:
        Baker Book House.

Bauer, Walter
    1979 *A Greek-English Lexicon of the New Testament*
        and other Early Christian Literature.
        2nd edit. Chicago: Univ. of Chicago Press.

Bornkamm, Gunther
    1971 *Paul.* New York: Harper & Row. (Trans. by
        D. Stalker).

Bruce, F. F.
    1972 *New Testament History.* Garden City:
        Doubleday & Co.

    1988 *The New International Commentary on the New*
        Testament--Acts. Grand Rapids: William B.
        Eerdman's Pub. Co.

Bryant, Coralie and Louise G. White
    1984 *Managing Rural Development with Small Farmer
          Participation*. West Hartford: Kumarian
          Press, Inc.

Bunch, Roland
    1982 *Two Ears of Corn*. Oklahoma City: World
          Neighbors.

Cassidy, Richard J.
    1987 *Society and Politics in the Acts of the
          Apostles*. Maryknoll: Orbis Books.

Drewery, Mary
    1979 *William Carey: A Biography*. Grand Rapids:
          William B. Eerdman's Pub. Co.

Gaertner, Dennis
    1993 *The College Press NIV Commentary--Acts*.
          Joplin: College Press Pub. Co.

Green, Michael
    1970 *Evangelism in the Early Church*. Grand
          Rapids: William B. Eerdman's Pub. Co.

Hamilton, Don
    1987 *Tentmakers Speak*. Ventura: Regal Books.

Harrow, G. J.
    1983 *The Ongoing Church*. Scarborough, OR:
          Everyday Pub. Co.

Hesselgrave, David J.
    1980 *Planting Churches Cross-Culturally*. Grand
          Rapids: Baker Book House.

Hock, Ronald F.
  1980 *The Social Context of Paul's Ministry:*
       Tentmaking and Apostleship. Philadelphia:
       Fortress Press.

Houston, James
  1989 *The Transforming Friendship.* Elgin, IL:
       Lion Pub. Co.

Hyden, Goran
  1983 *No Shortcuts to Progress: African Development*
       Management in Perspective. Berkeley: Univ.
       of California.

Kittel, Gerhard F. (ed).
  1971 *Theological Dictionary of the New Testament.*
       Vols 3,7. Grand Rapids: William B. Eerdman's
       Pub. Co. (Trans. by G. Bromiley).

Latourette, Kenneth S.
  1953 *A History of Christianity.* New York:
       Harper & Row.

Macgregor, G. H. C.
  1954 "Exegesis on the Acts of the Apostles," in
       The Interpreter's Bible. Vol 9. Ed. by
       George A. Buttrick. New York: Abingdon Press.

Moris, Jon R.
  1981 *Managing Induced Rural Development.*
       Bloomington: International Development
       Institute.

Murray, Andrew
  1952 *With Christ in the School of Prayer.*
       Westwood, NJ: Fleming H. Revell Co.

Norris, Frederick W.
    1984 "God and the Gods: Expect Footprints," in
          Unto the Uttermost, ed. by Doug Priest Jr.
          pp. 55-69. Pasadena: William Carey Lib.

Nouwen, Henri J.
    1976 *Reaching Out: The Three Movements of the
          Spiritual Life*. Glasgow: William Collins and
          Sons, Ltd.

O'Gorman, Frances
    1978 "Role of Change Agents in Development."
          East Lansing: Non-Formal Education Information
          Center. (Occas. Paper #3).

Paddock, Wesley
    1992 "Are Short-Termers the Future of Missions?"
          Christian Standard. 127:30:630-631.

Parker, T. H. L.
    1960 *The Dictionary of Theology*. Grand Rapids:
          Baker Book House.

Reapsome, James
    1993 "New Year's Liturgy." *Pulse*. 28:24:8.

Reese, Gareth L.
    1976 *New Testament History: A Critical and
          Exegetical Commentary on the Book of Acts*.
          Joplin: College Press Pub. Co.

Rosenblum, Mort and Doug Williamson
    1987 *Squandering Eden: Africa at the Edge*.
          San Diego: Harcourt Brace Jovanovich, Pubs.

Roseveare, Helen
    1987 *Living Faith*. Minneapolis: Bethany House.

Sine, Tom
1991 *Wild Hope.* Waco: Word Books Inc.

Stott, John R.
1990 *The Spirit, the Church and the World.*
Downer's Grove: InterVarsity Press.

Taylor, John V.
1972 *The Go-Between God.* New York: Oxford Univ.
Press.

Tucker, Ruth
1983 *From Jerusalem to Irian Jaya.* Grand Rapids:
Zondervan Pub. House.

Uphoff, Norman
1986 *Local Institutional Development: An
Analytical Sourcebook with Cases.* West
Hartford: Kumarian Press, Inc.

Willard, Dallas
1988 *Spirit of the Disciplines.* New York:
Harper & Row.

Willis, Avery T.
1977 *Indonesia Revival: Why Two Million Came to
Christ.* South Pasadena: William Carey Lib.

Wilson, J. Christy
1979 *Today's Tentmakers.* Wheaton: Tyndale House.

Wright, N. T.
1991 "One God, One Lord, One People: Incarnational
Christology for a Church in a Pagan
Environment." *Ex Audito.* 7:45-58.

Yamamori, Tetsunao
1987 *God's New Envoys.* Portland: Multnomah Press.

CPSIA information can be obtained at www.ICGtesting.com
Printed in the USA
BVOW010245240212

283727BV00001B/5/A